THE ROOTED PATH

The Rooted Path

Brittanie McQueen

Spireorbit
PUBLISHING

Contents

Disclaimer

Brittanie is a trauma-informed guide, student of Ayurveda, holistic healing, and creative/spiritual practices. She holds certifications in trauma-informed care and other non-licensed fields of study. Her work is intended for education, reflection, and personal growth. She is *not a licensed medical, mental health, or crisis professional*, and her offerings are *not a substitute for professional care*. She does not diagnose, treat, or prescribe. Always seek the guidance of a qualified provider for any medical or mental health concerns.

This book is for educational purposes only. It is *not intended to replace professional medical, psychological, or therapeutic advice*. The following examples are fictional and are meant to illustrate how the Rooted Path may look in different situations. While they are inspired by real patterns and experiences, the details have been changed or created for clarity.

Trigger Warning: This book explores themes of trauma, healing, and emotional intensity. Some passages may bring old memories, sensations, or unresolved experiences to the surface. Please move at your own pace. Take breaks when needed. If the content becomes overwhelming, pause and return only when you feel ready. You are not alone.

Healing is nonlinear. You are sovereign in how you walk this path. If you need immediate support, please reach out to a licensed therapist, medical provider, or crisis care resource in your area. Take what resonates. Leave what does not. Honor your well-being first, always.

For permissions, licensing inquiries, or training in The Rooted Path method, please contact:
ecoboundearth@gmail.com
www.ecoboundholistics.com

Acknowledgments

The Rooted Path grew first out of lived experience. Everything I share here began in my own body, as I learned to meet and transform the charges of stress, grief, and old wounds in real time.

Alongside that, I have studied Ayurveda, which shaped my understanding of energy, prana, and the ways the body and mind mirror nature's rhythms.

To broaden my perspective, I have also drawn on research in neuroscience, polyvagal theory, and somatic therapy. These fields offered language and validation for what I was already discovering in practice.

I am deeply grateful for the practitioners and traditions that have carried this wisdom forward. What you'll find here is not a replacement for those traditions, but a weaving of them into a framework that is personal, practical, and alive.

Introduction

This path began in my own body. I walked it before I named it. I didn't invent energy or the nervous system, I simply found my way through it. Only later did I realize it could serve others too. What I offer here is not a rigid system, but a framework you can adapt. Try it in your own way, at your own pace.

This book, and the work that spirals out from it, was born during a season of unraveling and sacred remembering. I began writing in a time when nothing made sense and yet, something beneath the surface began to stir. A whisper. A hum. A call to live differently, in rhythm with the Earth, in alignment with soul, and in reverence for beauty and truth. It didn't arrive all at once. It unfolded as I did.

Each page was written alongside my awakening, each chapter echoing not only what I know, but what I have lived, remembered, and become. This is not only a book. It is a path. A rooted path.

For years, I carried heaviness. Trauma sat like a stone in my chest, and every surge of emotion felt like drowning. Old wounds rose again and again, looping through memory, body, and breath until it seemed nothing would ever change.

But something shifted. Slowly, I discovered that within each wave of anger, grief, anxiety, or fear, there is also an opening. Emotions are not just storms to survive or problems to solve. Beneath each one runs a current, movement, life, possibility. When we meet that current with awareness, it can be transmuted into strength. This book was born from that discovery.

Many ancient traditions have long taught us how to meet energy as it rises through movement, breath, ritual, or mantra. But most of us were never shown how. What came to me felt like remembering something old. Something buried but still alive. This is not a theory. It is practice. It is permission.

Healing does not require us to transcend our bodies. It asks us to root into them. To feel the surge. To meet it with awareness. And from there, to transmute.

My focus in the Rooted Path is on the basics, meeting the surge of energy in the moment of impact. This book is for people who may be encountering this work for the first time. Over time, energy may appear not only as spikes but as ongoing sensations, and this is natural. The steps you learn here can help you to transmute energy at any stage of awareness.

Why This Book?

Every trigger releases a charge in the body, a spark that surges through the chest, the gut, the throat. I call it a charge, though you might think of it as a pulse beneath your skin or a jolt in your nervous system.

Most of us were never taught what to do with that charge. It either turns inward as shame and anxiety, or outward as conflict and harm. So much of what we're taught about healing is missing a crucial piece, how to meet the moment itself.

Therapy often looks backward, into the story of the past. Medicine often looks outward, toward diagnoses and prescriptions. Both hold value, but what's often missing is the now, the living moment when emotion surges and we can either lose ourselves or learn to ground ourselves.

Here is something rarely said, the body's healing depends on this rooting. Stress and trauma keep the nervous system in survival mode, blocking rest, repair, and even the immune system's ability to mend. Illness and fatigue linger when the body is never given the chance to calm, reset, and breathe. By meeting the charge in real time, we open the door for the body's own healing intelligence to flow again.

That is what this book offers, a practice for the moment of impact, when old wounds collide with the present.

The Rooted Path is not a theory or a set of borrowed practices. It is a living process that grew out of my own healing and awakening, a way of meeting emotional charge in the body and returning to a more rooted natural rhythm.

You don't need to be on a spiritual path to walk this one. The Rooted Path is for anyone with a body. Anyone who feels the surge of stress, fear, or old pain and longs for a way to meet it. Whether you call it energy, emotion, or simply overwhelm, the process works the same. Awakening may deepen the journey, but it isn't required to begin. This path is not about becoming someone else, but about remembering what has always been yours.

Along this path, you will learn to *activate* awareness in the very moment of charge, feeling the spark instead of being ruled by it. *Transmute* the surge by grounding it through breath, imagery, and elemental practices. *Integrate* the wisdom that rises once the storm has passed. *Embody* a steadier, freer self, no longer tethered by old trauma or hijacked by every obstacle. These are not abstract ideas. They are practices you can hold in the palm of your hand, even in the middle of a storm.

The Tree of Becoming

The next chapter will explain more in depth about the Tree of Becoming. This tree is more than an image, it's a way of seeing your own growth. It is what the Rooted Path grows into over time.

We begin by tending the roots: safety, steadiness, and choice. You will learn to listen for the quiet signals within you, to meet them without judgment, and to walk forward in a way that honors your pace.

The path will wait for you. Begin with lighter, newer charges, and let your strength grow before tending to the deeper roots. Name what you feel with kindness. A single word, a color, or a symbol is enough. The roots remember what the body already knows.

Keep a grounding stone nearby. Practice a grounding action you can return to at any time: feel your feet on the earth, hold something textured, take three slow breaths, or notice five things around you. Rest when you need to. The tree grows in seasons, and so do you.

This path also walks beside other forms of care. It does not replace therapy, medical support, or crisis care. If you need them, reach for them. If you walk alongside someone else, honor their pace. Begin and end each session with grounding, a breath, a touchstone, a vow.

The Rooted Path is not about escaping the body or overriding feelings. It is about remembering the body's truth that you are not broken, not fragile, not trapped. You are rooted. You are resilient. You are able to meet life as it comes and even transform it.

My hope is that as you walk this path, you will come to feel what I have felt, that no memory, no surge, no obstacle has the same grasp it once did. That you can face the storms of life with steadiness, not fear. The Rooted Path is an invitation to return to yourself, to trust your body's wisdom, and to walk in truth and light.

The Tree of Becoming, a living framework for body, mind, and spirit.

Part I – The Journey to the Rooted Path

One

The Tree of Becoming

The Rooted Path is where we begin. Roots are what hold us steady, what keep us nourished, what allow us to stand through storms. In this book, we focus on growing those roots, grounding in the body, meeting charge as it arises, and finding steadiness in the now.

The path does not end in the soil. From strong roots rises something more, the Tree of Becoming. This tree is not separate from you. It is you, your growth, your unfolding, your alignment with who you are meant to be.

Once you have steady roots, you start to build a new baseline or trunk. You become more resilient to these surges and they no longer overwhelm you. When your roots and trunk are steady, you are able to activate and align your mind, body, and spirit with much more ease.

When I speak of the Tree of Becoming, I am speaking of a way of seeing your healing as part of a living process. Too often we imagine healing as a destination, a fixed point we finally arrive at. Healing is more like growth, seasonal, changing, sometimes messy, and always alive. A tree does not grow all at once or in a straight line. It bends with the wind, deepens with the seasons, and expands slowly over time. In the same way, you are not required to "get it right" all at once. You are invited to root where you are, and let your becoming unfold in its own rhythm.

The roots of this tree are what we are tending throughout this book. They represent safety, steadiness, and choice. Without roots, a tree cannot draw nourishment from the soil or hold itself upright when storms come. In the same way, without grounding, we cannot truly heal. We may have insights or moments of peace, but they will not hold if we are not anchored. Roots are the foundation of all growth, and they are where your healing begins.

Some who walk this path will think of it as part of their spiritual awakening. Others will think of it as stress relief, trauma healing, or nervous system regulation. All are true. You don't have to carry the language of awakening to practice. The Rooted Path is not limited to mystics, healers, or seekers. It is a body practice, and bodies belong to everyone. If you breathe, you can root. If you feel, you can walk this path.

As you walk the Rooted Path, you are sending your own roots deeper. Every time you ground during a surge, every time you breathe into a charge instead of collapsing or lashing out, you are extending your roots. Over time, these roots give you access to strength you did not know you had. You will discover that storms that once toppled you now only rattle your branches. You will find that nourishment comes more easily, because your roots can reach deeper into the soil of your own life.

From the roots rises the trunk. The trunk is the steady center of your being, the structure that carries you upward. It represents the resilience that comes from living the practices of the Rooted Path. As you return to grounding again and again, you begin to notice a shift. You no longer feel as fragile, as easily thrown, as unstable. Instead, you carry yourself differently, with a kind of quiet strength. The trunk of your tree is your embodied center, the place within you that knows how to bend without breaking.

From the trunk extend the branches. These are the many directions your growth takes in life. Branches may represent your relationships, your work, your creativity, your service, or the ways you share your gifts with the world. When the branches are nourished by strong roots and a steady trunk, they can grow in balance. They reach outward and upward, connecting with others, offering shelter, or bearing fruit. Without roots, the branches wither. Without a trunk, they cannot stand. With a grounded foundation, your branches grow strong and flexible, reaching toward the light.

The leaves and fruit of your tree are the gifts of alignment. Leaves breathe life, they take in sunlight and transform it into nourishment. Fruit is what the tree offers to others, and to the world. In human terms, this is the way your healing ripples outward. As you learn to root and grow, your presence becomes a gift in itself. You may find that your relationships shift, that your creativity deepens, or that your way of being brings steadiness to others. The fruit of your tree may take many forms, words, art, compassion, service, or simply the quiet strength of being yourself without apology.

The Tree of Becoming reminds us that healing is not about shrinking into survival, but about expanding into wholeness. Many of us spend years trying to simply "get through" life, to manage symptoms, to control emotions. Life is not meant to be only survival. Like a tree, you are meant to grow, to reach, to bloom. Healing is not an end point, but the soil and water that allow your growth to unfold.

It is important to remember that growth happens in seasons. There will be times of blossoming, when everything feels alive and full of possibility. There will be times of shedding, when old patterns fall away and you feel bare. There will be winters, when growth seems hidden, and you wonder if anything is happening at all. Just as a tree is still alive in winter, drawing energy inward and deepening its roots, so are you. Growth is not always visible, but it is always present. Trust the seasons of your own becoming.

The Tree of Becoming also reminds us that healing is not only personal, but relational. Trees do not grow in isolation. They are part of forests, ecosystems, and communities of life. In the same way, your growth is supported by others, by loved ones, guides, healers, or friends who walk beside you. Just as trees share nutrients through their root systems, we share strength and wisdom through connection. You are not meant to heal alone.

In this book, we will stay close to the roots as we practice grounding, meeting charge in the body, and building steadiness. These practices are the soil of your growth. But know that as you root, you are already shaping your Tree of Becoming. Every breath, every moment of transmuted energy, every act of returning to yourself is part of a larger unfolding.

The branches, leaves, and fruit will come in time. You may not see them yet, but they are already within you, waiting for the season to arrive. Your work is to tend the roots, to care for the soil, and to trust that growth will happen as it is meant to.

The Tree of Becoming is not a destination, but a reminder that you are alive, growing, and that you are part of something larger. The roots you grow in this book will carry you into alignment with your body, mind, and soul moving together as one.

When you first begin, you may not feel the charges right away. At times, it may even seem like nothing is happening. But that, too, is part of the journey. The next chapter will explore why the signals of your body can feel hidden, what I call the fog, and how even through that haze, the call of your becoming still reaches you.

Two

The Fog and the Call

You don't need to have all the words to know something is shifting inside you. You don't even need to be certain what's wrong. It may not be loud or dramatic. It may not throw you off your feet or demand you stop everything.

Sometimes it's simply there, a subtle hum beneath the surface of your life, a quiet static you can't quite turn off. You might hear it only when the rest of the world grows still, as faint as wind in the leaves. It might show up as a tiredness that lingers no matter how much you sleep, or as a heaviness that follows you through the day, settling into your shoulders, your chest, or somewhere behind your eyes.

You may still be doing all the things you've always done, working, caring for others, showing up where you're needed, but beneath each movement there's a weight. It's the sigh you don't remember releasing. The way your body braces just before you speak. The pause before you say, "I'm fine," when a part of you isn't sure that's true.

Maybe you've tried to name it, burnout, anxiety, depression, overwhelm, trauma. Maybe you've been told this is just adulthood, and you nodded along, trying to accept it. But somewhere deep inside, a small voice wonders if this is really all there is. Not because you're expecting a grand miracle, but because however faintly, you can feel something else.

I call this state the fog. It isn't a diagnosis or a flaw, it's a lived experience of being half-here. Present but blurred, alert but unreachable, alive but slightly removed from your own life.

In the fog, edges soften. Emotions dull or lose their color. Hours slip by without accounting for them. Conversations feel distant, like they're happening through glass. Sometimes even your own body feels unfamiliar, as if you're watching it from a few steps away. You might catch yourself saying, "I just feel disconnected," or "I don't know who I am anymore."

And if you've been in the fog long enough, you might start to believe this is just who you are. I want to offer something gentler. You are not broken. You are under the fog, and that isn't you. It's just something around you, often born as protection. A shield that once kept you safe. A veil that softened what you could not yet bear.

Flashes Through the Fog

Even if the fog feels thick, you have likely already felt moments when something pierced through it. A sudden stillness before a storm. The split second your body tightened before the phone rang. The warmth in your chest when someone walked into the room and you knew they would matter to you.

These flashes are not imagination or coincidence. They are your body's oldest language, awareness arriving before the mind has words. In polyvagal science it's called neuroception, the nervous system sensing safety or threat faster than thought. In Ayurveda, it is the whisper of prana, the life force shifting beneath the surface.

You don't need to name it perfectly to know it's real. If you can remember even one of those moments, then you already know the fog isn't all there is. Something in you has always been awake, reaching for clarity, reminding you what it feels like to be alive.

The fog doesn't have to be your home forever. Beyond it, there is something more. For some, it comes like a jolt, a sudden sharp awakening. It's as if you've been walking through a dream and suddenly realize you're awake. For others, it's slower, a subtle tug at the edges of awareness. The faint pull of a current beneath still water.

It might arrive in small ways, a book you keep returning to. A phrase that catches in your chest and echoes for days. A conversation that leaves behind a warm hum long after the words have ended. Or it may come through your body, a refusal to keep moving in old patterns. A breaking point you can no longer ignore, or the quietest whisper saying, enough.

This is the wake-up call. It isn't a demand to burn your life down or to transform overnight. It's the deep, steady knowing that has never stopped listening, the pulse at the roots of your being, rising when something in you recognizes the truth and refuses to go back to sleep.

Even if it's only a whisper, even if you're not sure you trust it yet, it's there. The fact that you can feel it at all means you are still reachable. The call doesn't rush or shame you. It simply asks you to notice, to remain open, to let the possibility of another way take root.

When you do, something shifts, even if only slightly. The world may not look different, but you begin to meet it differently. You start to sense the moment between feeling and reaction, and in that space, a quiet invitation appears. What if I met this moment just as it is?

The wake-up call doesn't just wake you, it invites you onto a path. At first, it may feel like all you have is the awareness that something must change. As you keep answering, that awareness begins to take root.

What grows is not a straight road but a living path, roots reaching inward, branches reaching toward the light. This is what I call The Tree of Becoming, the shape of what happens when you keep showing up for the call, letting it shape you season after season.

The Tree of Becoming is not about fixing yourself. It's about meeting the raw currents of your emotions, sensations, and reactions with honesty, gentleness, and steady curiosity. As your roots deepen, your branches can bend with the wind without breaking. You begin to remember there has always been more to you than the fog allowed you to see.

Pause here. Feel your feet on the floor, your weight sinking down like roots. Notice one place in your life where you can remain steady, even as things shift. This is the first step. The wake-up call is not the end of the journey, but the opening of a door. You may not know what lies beyond or feel ready to step through. The moment you hear it, something in you is already moving.

At first, the path may feel hazy. You might take two steps forward, one back. You might circle the same ground, wondering if you're getting anywhere. This is part of it. The path isn't about rushing to a finish line, it's about allowing something deeper to grow.

You don't need to understand everything now. You don't even need to believe in energy or healing. You only need the willingness to keep breathing. To notice. To stay present, even one moment longer than yesterday.

If any of this resonates — the fog, the fatigue, the call, the stirring, then you are exactly where you need to be. Whether you are ready to step onto the path or still standing at its edge, the tree will meet you where you are. Something in you is reaching, like a root toward water, like a branch toward the light. Let it. Let it pull you, not with force, but with the quiet certainty that you are being called back to yourself.

In the chapters ahead, you'll learn how to meet yourself in that stillness, how to walk with the fog without losing your way, and how to grow into the steady, rooted presence that has been waiting within you all along.

Three

Listening for The Pulse

Beneath the bark of every living tree, movement flows unseen, sap rising and falling, water drawn up through the roots, tiny electrical signals passing from cell to cell. You may not hear it, but it's there, the pulse of life.

The human body is no different. Beneath thought, language, and the stories we tell about how we feel, a current moves through us. It shifts from moment to moment, responding to touch, memory, temperature, tone of voice, scent, movement, and even subtle changes in light or sound.

When this energy rises it means that this moment matters. In the Rooted Path, I call this rise in energy a *charge* or a *pulse*. Both names point to the same experience.

A sudden spark or a slow ripple, a signal the body sends when something within is touched, whether by joy, fear, longing, grief, or something else. It might arrive as subtly as the hush before a shift in the wind, or as powerfully as a flood through the senses. However it comes, it's always worth listening to.

How the Pulse Feels

The pulse rarely arrives with a clear label like anger, grief, or fear. Sometimes it's unmistakable, a surge of heat in the chest, sharp pressure behind the eyes, the prickling sensation of a nerve exposed. At other times, it's quieter, a tightening in the stomach, a downward pull as if gravity has grown heavier.

It might hum beneath the skin, trembling hands, or twitching jaw. Your voice may sharpen without warning, your breath may catch, your shoulders may rise before you even realize you're reacting.

Occasionally it's so faint it almost slips past unnoticed, a vague discomfort, a sense of being "off" without knowing why. Distraction, restlessness, or numbness may follow, not because anything obvious happened, but because something inside has shifted and the signal hasn't reached awareness yet.

The pulse is the body's language when words fall short. It isn't an enemy, and it isn't proof something is wrong. It's proof of life.

Pause for a moment. Notice one sensation in your body right now, maybe warmth, coolness, or tension. You don't have to change it, just notice. That noticing itself is the beginning of listening.

The Science of the Pulse

In scientific terms, the pulse reflects a shift in the nervous system. Electrical and chemical signals pass between the brain, body, and environment, moving faster than conscious thought.

The sympathetic branch prepares you for action, sometimes releasing adrenaline when it senses threat. The parasympathetic branch draws you toward rest and recovery. Both are part of the same system, and both serve to protect you.

In Ayurveda, the pulse is also seen as a movement of prana, the life force that animates all living beings. Prana flows through subtle channels called nadis and shifts in response to sound, memory, or sensation. You might notice it as warmth, coolness, expansion, contraction, heaviness, or lightness.

Even if the word energy feels unfamiliar, the experience does not. Your stomach drops after a sharp comment. Your heart flutters when someone you love enters the room. Heat rises to your cheeks in embarrassment. Your breath quickens before sharing important news.

That is the pulse, both science and mystery, nervous system and subtle body, chemistry and electricity, prana and physiology.

– A story from the path –

Each morning, a woman walks the same street to work. She notices sunlight filtering through leaves and the rhythm of her footsteps. One day, as she steps off the curb, someone brushes past too quickly. Her shoulders lift before she understands why. The moment passes, yet that evening her voice carries a quiet edge, an impatience she cannot name.

The Hidden Messages

Her body noticed first, and never stopped holding the moment. The pulse doesn't always arrive like a wave. Sometimes it's a thread woven through the day. Irritation in a conversation that drags on, the tightening in the throat when interrupted, the sudden urge to step outside without knowing why. These are not random. They are messages from your inner world, knocking softly on the door.

Some pulses are obvious, the flush of desire, the surge of protectiveness, the sting of betrayal. Others hide beneath layers of habit and self-protection. They may go unnoticed until much later, if at all. But even when quiet, they shape how you move through the world. They guide reactions, choices, and your sense of safety. They reveal your boundaries, your nourishment, your depletion.

If You Don't Feel Anything

If none of this sounds familiar, you are not broken, you are protected. Many people learn to go quiet inside to survive. Numbing may have been the only way to endure. Distance from sensation was once safe. This was not a weakness, it was wisdom.

If your pulse feels far away, it hasn't disappeared. It waits for the moment your system says, It's safe now. There's no need to chase or force it. The tree doesn't push its sap to rise in winter. It waits for the season to turn. Your body will, too.

Why Timing Matters

The brain protects not only from immediate danger but also from too much, too soon. That's why some memories blur, emotions stay distant, or healing feels stalled. This is not failure, it's pacing.

In trauma informed care, this is called staying within the window of tolerance. The range where you can feel and remain present.

In Ayurveda, it may be understood as tending to ojas, the vital reserves that must be strong enough to hold what is rising without depleting you.

When the pulse feels muted, your body may be conserving energy for the right time. This is love, not resistance.

Relearning the Language of Sensation

Most of us were never taught to feel without judgment. We were taught to explain, to justify, to make emotions reasonable. But the pulse doesn't speak in reason, it speaks in sensation. Relearning its language doesn't mean forcing fluency or turning every signal into a story. It begins with noticing.

Sometimes, when someone says, "I don't feel anything," what they really mean is "I don't know what to look for." Energy doesn't always feel like lightning or heat. Sometimes it's subtle. Sometimes it hides in plain sensation. Try this:

Hold out your hands.

Flex your fingers.

What do you notice? A stinging warmth? Tightening muscles? A buzzing? A tingling? That's energy. That's life moving through you. The same current that flows through emotion, through thought, through presence. If you can feel this, you can learn to feel everything.

You don't need to believe in chakras or prana. Just let your body show you. Start there. Start small. And then, keep noticing.

When you feel a flicker, a tightening, a lift in the chest, or a drop in the belly, pause. Remain for a moment. Let awareness sit beside the feeling as you would sit beside a friend who needs presence more than advice. Your roots will reconnect quietly, patiently.

At first, you may notice energy as a sharp spike, a surge of emotion or tension that comes and goes quickly. Over time, as you begin meeting it with awareness, you may also feel it as a steadier current that stays with you, a warmth in the chest, tingling at the crown, or a quiet presence that lingers. This too is natural. It is simply your body learning to stay open and hold more aliveness without shutting down.

A Small Practice for Meeting the Pulse

When something stirs within you (even faintly) pause. Notice where it rests in the body. Is it heat, pressure, coolness, stillness, or movement? Is it centered or spread out? Breathe into that place, not to change it but to let it know that you are listening.

The noticing itself is the shift. Each time you stay with a pulse without pushing it away or rushing to react, new pathways form in the nervous system. The body learns it can feel and stay without being swept away.

Over time, this becomes as natural as sensing the weather. You step outside and notice warm sun, cool wind, or heavy rain. Inside, you begin to sense the same, rising heat, quiet stillness, or slow expansion.

Whether the pulse surges like a storm or whispers like a breeze, it exists. Whether felt clearly or sensed only in absence, it is present.

The body remembers how to feel. The spirit remembers how to listen. The Tree of Becoming offers a way back, not through force or urgency, but through trust that what is ready will rise.

The pulse is more than a reaction, it's a messenger. Meeting it with gentleness transforms your relationship with life itself. And in that relationship, roots deepen. Branches grow supple. You remember yourself.

Four

A Fork in the Road

Sometimes the pulse does not appear as an idea or a practice at all, but as a moment that arrives in your own life. That is where my journey into the Rooted Path began.

It was late afternoon, the kind of light that softens everything it touches. The sun had lowered far enough that its glow was gold instead of white, and the edges of the table, the cup in my hand, and even my reflection in the window seemed to blur into the air.

That was when my phone lit up. Just a few words, ordinary words, but they were from... them. Before I could read it twice, my body had already decided something was happening. My chest tightened. My breath caught high in my throat. My stomach drew inward, knotting in a way I knew all too well. The reaction came fast and deep like a wave moving through me before I could choose. My pulse quickened and my muscles locked. My hands curled into fists without permission.

Within that heartbeat, I split in two. One part of me wanted to lash out, to say everything I hadn't said years ago, sharp enough to cut, precise enough to land.

The other part wanted to vanish, to delete the message, turn off the phone, pretend it had never arrived. I was caught between reaction and retreat, and both felt like survival.

The Body Decides First

None of this was about that text alone. My nervous system had recognized a pattern it had memorized long ago. It wasn't just a text. It was a mirror, reflecting every other time I'd been pulled into this loop.

Neuroscience explains moments like this. Parts of your brain can register a threat faster than conscious thought. In fractions of a second, signals trigger adrenaline and cortisol, muscles tighten, vision narrows, breath changes, and heart races.

Polyvagal theory describes this as moving between states: sympathetic activation (fight or flight) and dorsal vagal shutdown (freeze). In Ayurveda, it could be seen as prana rushing to the surface in defense, then contracting inward to conserve energy.

Even though my first impulse was to take one of the two familiar roads, to strike or to vanish, I paused. I noticed. That noticing was small and quiet, but it was the first root breaking through the surface.

The Two Roads

Most of us learn to handle activation in one of two ways, indulgence or suppression. Indulgence means feeding the pulse without question. The impulse rises and we let it choose for us. We say the words that land too hard. We send the message that feels righteous in the moment but tastes bitter later. We reach for the snack or pour the drink that numbs.

Suppression is just as common. The pulse rises, and we clamp down. We smile when we want to cry. We nod when we want to leave. We busy ourselves into silence. On the outside, it looks composed. Inside, it's a windowless storage room, every unfelt tremor stacking against the walls.

Both indulgence and suppression are survival strategies. They have their wisdom, but neither lets the pulse complete its cycle.

What Almost Worked

When I began to notice this pattern, I tried to interrupt it with every tool I could find: mindfulness, journaling, affirmations, breathwork, visualization, somatic exercises. Some helped. Many gave me insight. A few gave me temporary relief. But none truly changed the pattern in my body.

I could cry through an entire therapy session and still feel wired hours later, as if the energy had risen but not moved through. I could fill pages in a journal, trace my patterns to their roots, wrap them in compassion and still wake with the same knot in my ribs.

It wasn't that these practices were wrong. They were part of the path. They helped me to see. But they didn't yet teach me how to transform.

Over time, I began to see what was missing. Most approaches help you recognize the pulse. Some help you feel it. But very few teach you how to change it in real time, not in the mind alone, but in the body where it lives.

Until the energy shifts, the pattern stays. Recognition without integration keeps us circling the same tree, walking the same worn path.

The Subtle Shift

That day, I tried something different. I didn't lash out. I didn't shut down. I just stayed. My hands on my thighs, my breath shallow but steady enough, I turned toward the knot in my chest.

It wasn't my first time sensing energy. I had felt currents move through me before, lighter flows that rose and quieted on their own.

But this was different, the build-up was intense. I didn't know what to do and yet somehow, without training or prior knowledge of energy work, I did. It's like my body remembered something instinctual.

I breathed with it, stayed with it, and let it move downward, into the steadiness beneath me, into the ground that could hold what I could not. At that moment, it shifted. The energy didn't disappear, it quieted. And when it did, I felt stronger than I ever had before. The strength stayed. It became part of me.

This wasn't the beginning of my awakening. That had started long before, in quieter ways I couldn't yet name. But it was the first time I felt energy moving in my body this clearly, and that changed everything.

You may not feel it this way at first, and that's okay. Sometimes the shift is as simple as your jaw unclenching, your shoulders lowering, or your breath dropping lower in your chest. Sometimes it feels like warmth spreading or heaviness softening. However it arrives, the pulse doesn't stay frozen when you stay with it.

Right there, in my kitchen, with no witness but the quiet, I made a vow: I choose care. I choose no harm. Not just toward others, but toward myself.

It wasn't a vow of perfection. I knew I'd still react sometimes, still retreat sometimes. But it was a vow of return, a thread I could hold in my palm when the winds picked up.

The Ripples

Since then, I've seen this ripple through many lives. A woman stayed with the ache in her chest after a hard exchange with her sister, instead of replaying it for days. A mother held the heat of guilt after snapping at her child, instead of spiraling into shame. A teacher breathed with her anger after being dismissed in a meeting, instead of letting it spill into sharp words.

Each of them discovered what I had. You don't need to fix the charge. You only need to stay long enough for it to become something else.

That moment became the seed of what I now call the *Rooted Loop*, the living rhythm of the Path. Notice when the energy rises. Root by pausing and choosing how to hold it. Move with it, letting it shift into a steadier state. Seal the change, anchoring what you've learned.

It is not a quick trick or a rigid formula. It is a practice, one that deepens each time you walk it. Over time, the loop stops being something you "do" and becomes something you are.

Staying Is Becoming

You don't need to wait until you are calm to begin. You can begin in the swirl, in the ache, in the flood. The moment you choose to stay, you begin to change. Not because the storm disappears, but because your roots know how to hold.

That moment in my kitchen was not a dramatic breakthrough, no lightning strike or choir of voices. It was a quiet choice, a decision to remain with myself instead of abandoning my own ground.

Each time since, I've discovered something profound. The moment you stay, the moment you let the charge shift inside you instead of chasing or burying it, you begin to see more clearly.

The air feels different. The edges sharpen. The hum beneath the noise rises to meet you. Without trying, you start to notice the very first tremor of the pulse, the flash through the fog.

Five

Why Neither Road Leads to Peace

When strong feelings rise, most of us instinctively reach for one of two familiar roads: indulgence or suppression. Both may bring a moment of relief, but neither resolves what the body is carrying. They may look like opposites but both lead us back into the same loop.

Indulgence feels expressive, even cathartic in the moment. The words spill out, the drink is poured, the impulse is acted on. For a brief second, it feels like release.

But afterward? Regret, exhaustion, the weight of the same loop tightening. Each time you follow the pull without question, the body learns: when I feel this, I must act now. And the next time the pulse rises, it pulls harder.

Suppression looks calmer on the surface. You clamp down, smile when you want to cry, stay busy instead of letting yourself feel. On the outside, it seems composed. Inside, the body is still carrying it.

Suppressed energy doesn't vanish. It lodges in muscles, breath, digestion, and sleep. Stacked pulses build like layers of sediment until the smallest trigger sets them loose again.

Why the Body Does This

Your nervous system isn't failing you, it's protecting you. Constantly scanning for cues of safety or danger, it reacts faster than thought.

Polyvagal theory calls this neuroception the unconscious detection of safety or threat. In fight or flight, the body mobilizes. When you freeze, it withdraws. In fawn, it appeases.

Ayurveda describes the same pattern in a different language. Prana, the life force, surges to the surface when threatened, or contracts inward to conserve energy.

These are not flaws. They are ancient responses meant to keep you alive. But they were designed for short-term danger, not long-term living. When they become constant, you end up surviving your life instead of living it.

Why "Balance" Isn't Enough

Many healing approaches suggest a third road, balance. And balance has value. It widens your capacity to feel without being overwhelmed, helping you pause before reacting.

But balance is not the same as resolution. Often it means learning to carry the weight more comfortably rather than laying it down. Like adjusting the straps on a heavy backpack. It may be useful, but the backpack is still there.

True peace comes not from managing the load, but from emptying it. From letting the pulse complete its cycle so the body no longer has to brace against it.

The Cost of Bracing

Whether through indulgence, suppression, or even balance, bracing has a cost. Fatigue that doesn't match your day. Illness that lingers longer than it should. A short fuse, foggy memory, the feeling that emotions are either too much or too far away.

The surface circumstances change, a different partner, a different job, a different season but the same ache returns. Why? Because the pulse was never resolved. The roots remained pressed against the stone.

Imagine not having to carry the weight at all. Not shoving it down, not acting it out, not just holding it steady but letting it shift into something new.

Most healing paths point toward this truth, but few show you how to do it in real time, in the middle of the storm. Without that, it's easy to leave a therapy session, a ritual, or a ceremony cracked open but unsteady, stirred but not anchored. What's needed is a way to meet the pulse as it rises to allow the energy itself to change.

What Transmutation Really Means

Transmutation is not bypassing or "rising above." It is not smiling through harm or forcing yourself into forgiveness. It is the practice of staying present with the pulse, breathing with it, naming it, and allowing it space to move.

Grief may soften into love when it is fully felt. Anger, when met with steadiness, can reveal clarity. Longing, when held without running, can become presence instead of ache. On the Rooted Path, the pulse doesn't vanish. It transforms.

Begin With Noticing

The first step isn't to change anything. It's simply to notice. Think of the last time you felt something strongly. Did you act on it immediately? Did you bury it? Did you "handle it well" on the surface but still feel it echoing in your body hours later?

None of these are failures. They are maps, showing which road your body knows best right now. The moment you notice, you are no longer fully in the loop. You have a foothold in the soil.

You don't need to erase your pulse. You only need to meet it. And when you do, you may find that peace is not the absence of sensation, but the freedom to feel fully and still stay rooted.

That is where the real journey begins. That subtle difference, the flicker between outward and inward, is the same current that moves through a flash in the fog.

Why This Is the Root

What you just touched is the same awareness that catches the first pulse of a rising charge. We are not creating it from scratch. We are remembering it, rooting into it until it becomes second nature again. You don't have to understand it for it to be real. You only have to feel it.

In the chapters ahead, we will give it language, structure, and shape so you can return to it whenever you need, not as a rare accident, but as a living skill you carry for life.

Six

The Rooted Path Overview

A flash through the fog is the first glimmer, the way your body says something is here before the mind decides what to do with it. The Rooted Path begins in that glimmer.

It's not a quick fix or a clever trick to *hack* your emotions. It's not about muscling your way into calm or pretending you don't feel what you feel.

It's the art of noticing that first pulse, the knot in your stomach, the pulse in your throat, the ache in your chest, and staying with it just long enough to let it show you something new.

And for those who have begun the journey of awakening, this is where the two paths meet: the grounded, physical skill of tending the nervous system, and the quiet, luminous awareness that rises when you stay present in the center of your being.

It's certainly not about standing at the edge of your storm and then deciding between two false extremes. Unleashing all your emotion until it scorches the ground, or burying it so deep it hardens into something you can no longer name.

The Rooted Path is something different, quieter, slower, and infinitely more alive. It doesn't demand that you understand every layer of what you're feeling before you begin. It doesn't require you to be healed, whole, or certain.

It only asks, Can you linger for one more breath, one heartbeat longer than you usually do and notice? Can you let the energy move inside you before you react, suppress, or disappear into distraction? Can you let it speak in the language of sensation, image, and knowing, even if you can't yet translate it? That is the beginning of the Rooted Path.

The Middle Space

We have all lived caught between two roads. Indulgence, where we react, vent, spiral, explode. Or suppression, where we freeze, numb, avoid, distract. Both are survival strategies. Both have, at times, saved us but neither one truly brings peace.

The Rooted Path is a middle space. It doesn't ask you to feed the charge, but it also doesn't ask you to starve it into silence.

It invites you to hold it, to stay present without being overtaken. To let the energy shift in your body before it turns into harm, toward yourself or anyone else.

And if you are on a spiritual path, this middle space is the fertile ground between thought and action, where the soul has space to breathe, and the truth beneath the reaction can rise like water from a deep well.

This isn't about being calm all the time. It's about knowing how to return to calm after the chaos has passed.

It's about creating a living pathway inside yourself, a rooted track through the forest of your being so that when a storm comes, you can find your way back. So you can remember, I don't have to abandon myself to survive this.

Why It Works

When something happens, a sharp email, a sudden rejection, a fear that clutches at your ribs, a boundary crossed, your body responds before you have time to think.

Two systems come alive in the same breath. Your nervous system, shifting into a survival state (fight, flight, freeze) through a process called neuroception, the unconscious detection of safety or threat.

Your energy body, changing in ways you can feel, your field contracts or expands, your breath catches or deepens, your muscles tighten, your gut twists, your hands heat or tremble.

Together, these create your state, the combination of physiological, emotional, and energetic signals that color your moment.

If you don't know how to meet that state, you'll fall into your oldest patterns. Not because you're broken, but because your body is doing its best to protect you with the tools it already knows. The truth is, your body is meant to adapt. And energy, by its nature, is meant to move. When you guide it skillfully (not forcefully) it begins to change shape.

That is why the Rooted Path works, it meets the energy exactly as it is, without shame, without rushing, and gives it a safe container to soften, shift, and return to flow.

And for the awakened traveler, it also clears the space for higher insight to reach you without distortion. The more fluidly your body can shift, the more clearly the deeper current of your life can be felt.

Contain. Soften. Transform.

Imagine pouring boiling water into a paper cup. The cup warps, buckles, collapses. Pour that same water into a clay mug, and it holds. It even cools the water over time. Your nervous system is the container.

When you meet your charge with fear or force, it spills everywhere, into words you can't take back, into muscles that stay locked for days.

But when you meet it with grounded posture, slower breath, anchored attention, you become the clay mug. The heat doesn't need to be extinguished. It only needs to be held.

Physiologically, this is the moment the vagus nerve engages, sending the signal: We are safe enough now to settle. Your heart rate slows. Your amygdala (the brain's alarm bell) quiets.

Your prefrontal cortex, the part of you that can choose instead of react, comes back online. And the energy? It responds. It softens. It spreads. It smooths.

When the energy softens, so do you, not because you forced yourself into peace, but because peace became possible.

And in that peace, if you are listening, you may hear the whisper beneath the noise, the one that has been waiting to speak to you all along.

Transformation, Not Control

Here's the part most people miss, The Rooted Path is not about controlling your feelings. Control is exhausting, like holding a beach ball under water. You can do it for a while, but the moment you slip, it bursts up to the surface with even more force.

Transformation is different. Transformation is letting the air out. It's changing the form of the energy so it no longer needs to be managed at all.

Control keeps the charge exactly as it is, only hidden. Transformation changes the charge itself, and in doing so, changes you.

— A story from the path –

Someone once told me, their anger felt like a volcano. "It either explodes, or I bury it until I hate myself." When they tried the Rooted Path, they didn't try to "calm down" or tell themself not to be angry.

They imagined the lava cooling instead of erupting.

They pictured the heat becoming solid stone, strong, grounded, and unshakable. They breathed, stayed, felt. Within minutes, the pressure in their chest eased. They didn't need to yell. They didn't need to swallow their truth. The energy had shifted, and so had they.

They were not drained or detached. They were rooted.

For those attuned to awakening, moments like this are not just emotional victories, but spiritual ones. Each transformation is a clearing of the lens, allowing you to see and respond from the deepest, clearest part of yourself.

Not Just Transmutation, Integration

Shifting your energy is powerful. But it's only the middle of the story. Without integration, the change is temporary. You'll feel lighter for a while but return to the same patterns next time. Integration is what teaches your body that this is our new baseline now.

In the Rooted Path, we don't just meet the charge and soften it, we anchor the new state. We let it land in the nervous system, in the breath, in the cells.

We seal it with a gesture, a word, a pause. We live in it for a few minutes, long enough for the memory to imprint. Every time you complete the loop, your body remembers, and that becomes who you are.

For the spiritual traveler, integration is what allows insight to become embodiment. Without it, even the clearest revelation fades. With it, each awakening settles into the roots of your being, changing how you walk in the world.

Growing Your Root System

Every time you choose this path instead of the old roads, you send down another root. Some roots are tiny, a single breath in the middle of a tense conversation. Some are deep, a full cycle of noticing, holding, and transforming.

Over time, those roots interlace into a living foundation. They hold you even in the biggest storms. They keep you steady when the wind rises.

Roots are not built in a day. They grow choice by choice, moment by moment, until the Path is not just something you remember, it is something you stand on.

And when life shakes you, it is those roots that keep you upright, and for some it is in that steadiness that the sacred becomes clear.

Part II – Walking the Path Step by Step

Seven

The Four Steps of the Rooted Path

The Rooted Path is not a set of rules. It's a living rhythm you can return to whenever your body carries more than it can comfortably hold.

It could be anger. It could be grief. It could be the dizzy hum of anxiety or even an overwhelming joy. Whatever the charge, this path isn't about control, escape, or ignoring your feelings until they fade.

It's about meeting the energy with care and guiding it into a form you can live with, one that doesn't harm you, others, or your future self.

This isn't a quick fix or a one-time technique. It's a way of being with yourself that honors your biology, your energy's natural flow, and your deepest values. Every time you walk it, you remind your system, "I can feel fully and still remain steady."

Step One: Activate

Before you can guide energy, you must first meet it exactly as it is. Most people rush past this part, not because they want to, but because the sensations of activation feel like the problem.

Your heart races. Your breath shortens. Your shoulders lift. Your mind starts telling the story, but activation is not the enemy. It's the doorway.

Here, you simply notice the charge, not to analyze, but to recognize it as energy moving through your system. Name the sensation instead of the story.

I feel heat in my chest. I feel pressure in my throat. This naming creates a small gap between reflex and choice.

Biologically, it re-engages your prefrontal cortex, the part that can choose instead of react. Energetically, it shows you're willing to stay with yourself.

Step Two: Transmute

Once the charge is acknowledged, it becomes workable. Transmutation is the alchemy of turning raw, reactive energy into something you can hold. You're not forcing it to vanish, you're giving it a shape and a path to move.

This might be slowing your exhale, seeing the fire in your chest become a steady ember, pressing your feet into the ground until the excess current drains, humming until the vibration softens.

When your body feels safe enough to stay with activation without being overwhelmed, the nervous system naturally completes the cycle. The jaw unclenches. The flutter in the belly steadies. The lump in the throat melts into a slow breath.

You're not calming by force, you're letting the energy become what it was always meant to be: movement, warmth, release, flow.

Step Three: Integrate

Without integration, the shift is temporary. Integration teaches your whole system: This is our new baseline now. It's both physical settling and intentional remembering.

Physically, you pause after the shift. Let your body register the difference, dropped shoulders, slower breath, a clearer mind. Intentionally, you mark it with a gesture, a breath, or a phrase, "I choose care. I am safe to feel."

Neuroscience calls this state-dependent learning, the brain encodes experiences more deeply when you notice them in real time. Spiritually, it's planting a root in new soil.

Step Four: Embody

Embodying means carrying the shift into your next conversation, your next choice, your next moment.

It's one thing to find calm after the storm. It's another to keep even a thread of that rootedness when the next wave hits. This is where your nervous system begins to expect safety as a possibility, not just threat.

You might notice yourself pausing before you reply to a difficult message. You might hear your breath steadying without having to think about it. You might feel your body return to center on its own. Over time, the path stops being something you "do" and becomes something you live.

Why These Four Steps Work Together

Activate – turn toward the truth of what's rising.

Transmute – give that truth a new shape.

Integrate – root the shift into your system.

Embody – carry it into your life.

Miss a step, and the shift is partial. Walk them all, and you create the conditions for deep, lasting change. This isn't "thinking your way" into peace, it's letting your nervous system rewire, your energy return to flow, and your inner roots grow stronger with each loop you walk.

A Simple Reminder

You don't have to do this perfectly. Some days you'll skip a step or get lost in it. That's still the path. The Rooted Path is not a performance, it's a return. Every loop strengthens your roots. Every pause in the middle of a surge teaches your system, I can meet myself here. When you can meet yourself here, you can meet anything.

Eight

Activate

Activation is the moment the current begins to move. It doesn't ask for your permission, and it rarely arrives at a convenient time.

Sometimes it appears as a gentle ripple across still water. Other times, it strikes like a wave crashing at your feet before you've even seen it coming. You might feel your heart quicken, your chest tighten, or your thoughts sharpen or scatter. Your body may lean forward, ready to confront, or curl inward ready to hide.

For most of us, this is the point where we either react or retreat. We fire back the text, slam the cupboard, and defend or explain ourselves in a rush of urgency. Or we shut it all down, burying the feeling under "I'm fine" while our bodies quietly carry the weight.

On the Rooted Path, we approach this moment differently. Instead of being swept into old reflexes, we pause. We name what is happening. We let it be here without running from it or trying to crush it.

Activation as the Doorway

We are often taught to see activation as the problem, the part we must get rid of as quickly as possible. Activation itself is not harmful, in fact, it's your body doing exactly what it was designed to do.

Biologically, your autonomic nervous system has detected something it considers important: a possible threat, a potential opportunity, or a meaningful change in your environment. In response, the sympathetic branch of your nervous system may fire up (the fight-or-flight response) to give you the energy to act. Or, if your body senses overwhelm, the dorsal vagal branch may begin pulling you toward shutdown (the freeze response). Either way, your body's intention is the same, to protect you.

Energetically, the process mirrors this. In Ayurveda, you might describe it as prana surging to prepare you for movement.

In Traditional Chinese Medicine, it could be qi rushing to address an imbalance. In the language of subtle energy, your field may contract or flare in response to change, memory, or resonance.

The problem is not activation itself, it's the learned patterns of either drowning in it or rushing to make it disappear before we have heard what it has to say.

Why It Happens in "Small" Moments

One of the most frustrating parts of activation is that it doesn't always match the size of the moment. A sideways comment from a coworker can trigger the same chest-tightening as a major conflict.

A minor change in plans can spark the same restlessness as a real loss. This isn't because you're "too sensitive," it's because your nervous system doesn't measure importance the way your thinking mind does.

Your body's response is based on patterns learned over a life-time, not on the logic of the present. If something feels even faintly like a past hurt or a previous danger, your system will light up.

It's an echo, and your body errs on the side of overreacting be-cause, in evolutionary terms, that's what kept our ancestors alive. It was safer to mistake a stick for a snake than to miss the real snake entirely.

The other reason activation can feel so big is that it com-pounds. If we don't have a way to let the charge move through us, it stacks in the body, a hundred unprocessed tensions adding weight to the one in front of us. This is why a "small" moment can feel like it tips you over the edge. You're not just feeling today's surge; you're feeling the stored energy of many moments your body didn't get to complete.

The truth is, we were built to transmute this charge. Our sys-tems evolved with movement, shaking, breath, sound, natural ways of discharging energy after stress. Animals do it instinctively.

Humans still can, but cultural conditioning has trained us to suppress, ignore, or rush past these releases. The Rooted Path is about remembering this original capacity and reclaiming it as a skill.

From Fog to Feeling

If you've been living in what I call the fog, that state of discon-nection from your own sensations, activation can be hard to no-tice. The fog dulls your awareness until you only realize you were upset long after the fact, when your shoulders ache or your stom-ach has tied itself into knots.

Step One is not about suddenly feeling everything with full intensity, it's about catching the first thread you can find. That thread might be the realization that your breath has become shallow, or that you've stopped hearing the background sounds in the room.

It might be the faintest heat in your chest, or the subtle tightening of your jaw. If even that feels out of reach, start smaller still. Touch your own hand and feel the texture of your skin. Notice your feet on the floor and the way the surface supports you.

These simple acts are like gently knocking on the door of sensation. With time, and repetition, the door will begin to open.

Awareness Before Action

Activation is not about making yourself more worked up; it's about allowing yourself to register what is already happening. Instead of leaping into the mental story, they're ignoring me again, this always happens, I can't trust anyone, you slow down. Slow enough to notice, my stomach feels tight, my jaw is clenched, my palms are warm. You are turning toward sensation rather than away from it.

This shift from story to sensation changes everything. When you're caught in the story, you are either replaying the past or projecting into the future. When you are anchored in sensation, you are fully in the present moment.

Neuroscience shows that this engages the insula, the part of the brain that tracks your body's internal state. The more often you practice this, the earlier you will catch activation, and the more choice you'll have about what comes next.

The Activation Pause

One practical way to meet activation is what I call the Activation Pause. The moment you sense something shifting, a tone in someone's voice, a tightening in your belly, a spark of irritation, stop for just a breath.

Name the sensation in purely physical terms, "Heat in my face," or "Shoulders lifting." Keep your attention on one area of the body where the feeling is strongest, letting everything else fade into the background for now.

Finally, drop the timeline, you are not thinking about when this happened before or what might happen next. You are simply here, with what is rising right now. Four steps, four breaths, enough to begin creating space.

The Power of a Micro-Yes

I think of this act of staying with activation as a micro-yes, a small but profound agreement between you and your body. It isn't a sweeping, romantic Yes to everything life throws at you, and it certainly isn't pretending to enjoy discomfort.

It's a simple, deliberate willingness. Yes, I will feel this for one more breath. Yes, I will keep my hands open instead of curling them into fists, for now. Yes, I will give this sensation the dignity of my attention.

Each micro-yes plants another root. Over time, those roots grow strong enough to hold you steady in the midst of storms.

Common Missteps

There are a few patterns that can pull you away from the heart of this practice. One is jumping to meaning too quickly.

You notice a tightening in your chest and immediately conclude it means you're unsafe, unworthy, or in danger.

Another is trying to fix the sensation right away, using deep breathing or self-talk to make it go away before it's had a chance to settle naturally. This can actually teach your system that the feeling is intolerable, which reinforces the cycle.

And finally, in some spiritual circles, activation is mistaken for "bad energy" that must be cleared immediately. I want you to know that activation is not a flaw, it is simply movement.

Everyday Examples

Activation shows up in all kinds of moments. You might feel it when you receive a sharp email, as your shoulders tense and your jaw sets.

Instead of firing back a quick reply, you pause to feel your hands resting on the keyboard. Or when you are waiting for medical results and your stomach flips, you resist the urge to scroll your phone to numb the sensation, and instead notice the flutter in your belly and the faint shake in your fingers.

In grief, activation might appear as a tightening in your throat when a certain song plays; you simply place your hand there and breathe.

Even in joy, activation can be present, like when your child runs toward you laughing and your chest floods with warmth. In creativity, it may come as a tingling in your scalp when inspiration strikes.

In every case, the first step is to notice.

– A Story from the Path –

A woman believed she was bad at feeling her feelings. She would either cry until she was wrung out or shut down entirely.

She focused on nothing but Step One for several weeks.

Then one day, during a tense conversation with her teenage son, she felt the rush begin, her heart pounding, her face heating.

Instead of telling herself, He's being disrespectful or I need to calm down before I say something I regret, she silently named, Heat in my cheeks. Pulse in my neck.

She didn't try to change it or slow her breath; she just noticed. Later, she told me, "It was like I had a foothold on a cliff. I still had to climb, but I didn't feel like I was falling anymore."

That foothold is exactly what activation offers. You don't have to be calm to begin. You don't have to have the whole storm handled. You simply need to be willing to turn toward the first drop of rain. Activation is that turn, the beginning of meeting yourself in the moment.

Nine

Understanding Energy

Before we can work with transmuting energy, we need to understand what we are actually engaging with. The word energy means very different things depending on who you ask.

To a physicist, it's the capacity to do work, the potential and kinetic forces that move the universe. To a doctor, it's the ATP produced in your cells, the tiny chemical packets that keep you alive. To an acupuncturist, it's qi flowing through meridians. To an Ayurvedic practitioner, it's prana moving through the nadis. To someone in the middle of a panic attack, it's the restless, unshakable current rushing through their body.

The truth is, all of these are true at the same time. The Rooted Path works because it meets energy on every level, physical, emotional, mental, and subtle.

The Energy Within

At its most tangible, your body runs on bioelectricity. Every nerve impulse is an electrical signal. Every heartbeat is a small surge of current. Every muscle contraction depends on the movement of charged ions across cell membranes. Metabolism transforms glucose and oxygen into ATP, the molecular "battery" that powers all life processes. Without this constant exchange, you wouldn't move, think, digest, or breathe.

Energy is more than chemical fuel. It is movement and expression. Emotions themselves are energy in motion, a truth hidden in the word e-motion. Joy might feel like an upward, expanding warmth in your chest. Fear can feel like a quickened pulse and a pulling back in the belly. Anger might bring heat to your face and a forward push in your shoulders. Grief often arrives as a heaviness in the ribcage, a downward pull in the whole body.

These sensations are not imaginary; they are measurable shifts in heart rate, breathing rhythm, hormone levels, and electrical activity in the nervous system.

Ancient traditions mapped them long before modern science could measure them. In Ayurveda, the vital current is prana (life force) moving through channels called nadis, nourished by breath, food, thought, and environment. When prana is strong and balanced, you feel alive, steady, and clear; when it is blocked or depleted, you feel fatigued, disconnected, or unwell.

Traditional Chinese Medicine describes this same principle as qi, flowing through meridians and feeding every organ and tissue. Stagnation of qi from stress, trauma, or overexertion, can lead to pain or illness, while restoring flow restores health.

Modern research is beginning to confirm what these traditions have always known. Emotional and physical health share the same current, and both depend on movement, rhythm, and balance.

The Energy Field Around You

Your energy is not contained by your skin. Every living thing radiates an electromagnetic field, measurable, though still not fully understood.

The human heart produces the largest field in the body, extending several feet in every direction. Its patterns shift with your emotional state, a fact measurable through changes in heart rate variability. The brain produces its own smaller, detectable field as well.

This field is in constant conversation with your surroundings. You might feel heaviness walking into a room where people have just argued, even before a word is spoken.

Sitting beside someone calm and grounded can naturally slow your breathing. A hug from someone you love may bring an involuntary exhale.

Many traditions call this surrounding energy the aura or subtle body, a luminous field layered around the physical body.

While science does not confirm every detail of ancient descriptions, research in psychophysiology and social neuroscience shows we do sense and respond to the states of others, even without words or conscious awareness.

The Energy Between Us

Energy does not just move within individuals, it moves between them. Your nervous system is part of a social nervous system, wired to attune to others. This is why a baby calms when held by a relaxed parent, why laughter spreads through a group, and why panic can ripple through a crowd before anyone fully understands what's wrong.

Polyvagal theory calls this neuroception, the unconscious detection of safety or danger through tone of voice, eye contact, or the rhythm of movement.

On a larger scale, entire communities can share an energetic tone. During collective grief, the air can feel heavy. During celebration, the atmosphere can feel electric.

Sacred spaces often carry a stillness beyond ordinary quiet. The HeartMath Institute has even explored how human emotional states may influence the Earth's magnetic field, and how changes in that field might influence us in return.

Whether or not we accept the planetary scale, we have all felt the local version, the shared hush before a curtain rises, or the unity of a crowd chanting for a cause.

What This Means for the Rooted Path

When you feel activation it might not be only yours. You may be resonating with another person's field, picking up on the emotional tone of a space, or even carrying echoes of a collective mood. Your own story may be just one thread in a much larger weave.

This perspective changes how we hold our experience. It reminds us that what we feel is real, but not everything we feel necessarily originates with us.

It gives permission to approach energy with curiosity rather than judgment, and to ask, what part is mine? What part belongs to the space I'm in?

Most importantly, it shows that when you transmute your own energy, you also shift the field you are part of. Your steadiness ripples outward. Others feel it, even if they cannot name why.

Energy Without the Labels

You do not need to believe in meridians, chakras, or magnetic fields to walk the Rooted Path. You only need to notice that your body responds to life in real, physical ways, and that those responses can change.

Call it qi, prana, bioelectricity, emotional current, or simply "what I'm feeling right now." The name doesn't matter, because the principles are the same. Energy wants to move, complete its cycle, and transform.

A Bridge to Transmutation

This chapter is the bridge between Activate and Transmute. Without a sense of what energy is, how it moves, how it layers, how it connects us, the idea of transmutation can seem abstract or forced.

With this understanding, you can see that energy is never fixed or singular; it is alive. Transmuting energy is not about suppressing a reaction or forcing yourself into calm. It is about engaging with life-force movement directly and guiding it into a form that serves you, others, and the space you share.

The Rooted Path is personal, but it is never only personal. Every shift you create in your own field is a quiet offering to the greater field we all live within.

In the upcoming chapter we will discuss what transmutation is and how to transmute energy even if you do not feel it in your body.

Ten

The Nature of Transmutation

Transmutation is not control. It is not suppression. It is not the false calm of pushing something down until it stops moving.

Control and suppression both rest on the belief that the energy rising in you is a threat, something to dominate, override, or erase. They demand tension. They keep the nervous system braced, shoulders lifted, jaw tight, and mind on guard.

If you hold that tension long enough, it eventually leaks, bursts, or collapses inward. Sometimes it comes out sideways, in irritability toward the wrong person, in exhaustion that feels like illness, in a creeping sense of detachment. Other times it explodes directly, in words you regret or actions you cannot take back.

Transmutation begins with a completely different belief. The energy itself is not the enemy. Energy is alive. It carries information. When it is met with skill and care, it can change form, shifting from something that hijacks you into something that supports you.

Energy Is Living

Every tradition that works with the body, from Ayurveda's prana, to Chinese Medicine's qi, to modern somatic therapy's awareness of activation, agrees on one truth: energy moves. It is meant to move. It is not meant to freeze in place or loop endlessly, circling in your system without release.

When you feel a knot in your stomach, a buzzing in your chest, or heat rising in your neck, you're not just experiencing "stress" in the casual sense. You are feeling the body's current, a physiological and energetic cascade.

Biologically, this is your nervous system shifting gears, heart rate adjusting, hormones releasing into the blood, and muscles tightening or loosening. Energetically, it is a change in your field, an expansion, contraction, or pulse of life force moving to a place it's needed (or getting stuck where it cannot flow onward).

Sometimes this current rises in protection. Sometimes it comes in grief. Sometimes it arrives as joy too big to contain. The problem is not that energy appears, its presence means you are alive.

The challenge is how we meet it. When we meet it with fear, we inflame it. When we meet it with force, we shut it down. In both cases, the energy loses its natural intelligence. By *intelligence*, I mean that energy is not random; it carries something to teach us. When transmuted, it retrains the body in how to respond. The charge can flow, the nervous system can calm, and over time the body can begin to heal from all the years of suppression or indulgence.

From Fog to Feeling

For many, especially those who have lived through trauma or prolonged stress, the idea of feeling energy can seem distant. Instead of heat, hum, or movement, there may be nothing at all. Just fog. Flatness. A vague sense of going through the motions.

This is not failure. It is the nervous system's wisdom. Fog is a form of protection, the body's way of saying, "If we don't feel too much, we can't be hurt too much."

The first step out of fog is not to force clarity, but to invite noticing. Begin with the smallest, safest cues. The weight of your body in the chair, the temperature of the air on your skin, the rhythm of your breath without changing it, the texture of the floor under your feet.

These micro-acts of attention are reintroductions, each one telling your system, it's safe to be here. It's safe to notice again. Over time, the fog thins, sensations return, and you can work with energy directly, not as an abstract idea, but as something you feel moving within you.

The Role of Intention

By its nature, energy is neutral. The same rush of activation in your chest could turn into an outburst of anger or fuel a passionate defense of someone you love.

The same churn in your belly could spiral into anxiety or sharpen your attention for something that matters. The raw energy doesn't determine the outcome, your relationship to it does.

Intention is the pivot point. When you transmute, you aren't erasing the energy, you are inviting it into a new role. You decide what you want it to become.

You might ask, do I need this energy to settle into clarity? Can I root it into the ground as steadiness? Could this grief become compassion? Could this rage become a fire that fuels my boundaries without burning me from the inside?

Naming your intention gives the energy direction. Without direction, energy drifts; with direction, it becomes something sacred.

Transmutation Does Not Erase

One of the most persistent myths about healing is that the goal is to make uncomfortable sensations disappear. But if you erase the energy, you erase part of what makes you alive.

Transmutation does not make energy vanish, it changes its expression. The tightness in your chest might become warmth. The restless hum in your belly might become a steady current that moves you forward instead of scattering you.

The sharp heat in your throat might soften into a steady voice. The memory of what was there may remain, but its weight, charge, and grip will be different. You will no longer brace against it, you will carry it with ease.

If you feel a small charge now, place one hand on your chest and take a slow breath. Imagine the breath wrapping gently around that feeling, giving it just enough space to soften.

Ritual as a Bridge

When you are first learning to transmute, the process can feel abstract. How do I "shift" energy if I can't see it? How do I know when it's done? This is why we begin with ritual.

Ritual makes the invisible visible. It gives your body and mind something tangible to hold while the energy changes shape. A ritual is a container, like a clay mug that holds boiling water until it cools.

When you light a candle, pour water into a bowl, press your hands into soil, or speak your intention into the wind, you give your nervous system a clear signal, this is the moment we begin.

The external act grounds the internal shift. Over time, your body will learn the shape of that shift so well that you'll be able to create it without the full ritual, simply by recalling the vow, movement, or breath.

Why Ritual Works

On the scientific level, embodied cues like touch, movement, and breath activate sensory pathways that calm the nervous system and signal safety to the brain. Symbolic actions give your mind a coherent narrative. This is how we move from one state to another. Repetition creates neural pathways that make the shift easier and faster over time.

On the spiritual level, ritual honors the living nature of energy. It treats the shift as a sacred act rather than a mental exercise. It creates a dialogue between your inner and outer worlds, with intention inside mirrored by expression outside. When using ritual for release or transmutation it is very important to speak with intention.

Words carry resonance. When spoken aloud, they give shape and vibration to what lives within you. To name something is to draw it from the unseen into the seen, from the felt into the tangible.

Without intention, words can scatter or even reinforce the very patterns you're trying to release. With intention, words become aligned, they steady the mind, focus the body, and direct energy toward healing.

Speaking with intention is not about saying the "right" words, but about letting your voice match your truth. It is the difference between repeating empty phrases and speaking a vow your whole being stands behind. When words, breath, and awareness move together, they create a channel through which energy can truly shift.

Speaking with Intention

Intention for *Release*: When a surge feels heavy or overwhelming, place your hands on the ground or on a stone and speak aloud: "I release what no longer serves me. I root into what is steady and true. May this energy return as strength and light."

Intention for *Grounding*: When you feel unsteady or scattered, stand with both feet planted and say: "I root into this moment. I belong here. I am safe to breathe and be."

Intention for *Calling In*: When you want to invite strength, clarity, or peace, lift your palms upward and whisper: "I welcome what nourishes me. I call in what is steady and true. May this energy guide me forward."

Your words don't need to match mine, these are just examples. The most powerful words are the ones that rise naturally from your own heart. What matters is that they carry your truth. Speak simply, speak honestly, and with intention. Let your voice align with what you mean.

Once you grow comfortable speaking with intention, you can begin to weave those words into ritual. Ritual makes energy movement more tangible. I began with ritual myself, long before I could feel energy directly in my body. It allowed me to release built-up emotions so they could flow outward instead of stagnating.

From Training Wheels to Trust

At first, ritual is like training wheels, offering stability while you learn to balance. As you practice, the shift begins to live in your body.

You might close your eyes in a meeting and feel the cooling water you once poured, stand in a crowd and recall the vow you once spoke into the wind, or feel your feet on the earth and remember the stone you once held as your anchor.

This is when transmutation becomes portable, something you can do anywhere, without tools or special settings. But it begins with something you can touch, see, and feel.

The Four Elemental Pathways

In the chapters ahead, we'll explore four elemental approaches to ritual:

Fire — transformation through release and change

Water — cleansing, flow, and softening

Earth — grounding, stability, containment

Air — clarity, movement, lightness

Each one begins with a vow or blessing that names what the energy is now and what you wish it to become. These elements are not magic tricks, they are mirrors reflecting a truth about how energy moves in the body and in the world. You may be drawn to one more than the others, and that's natural. Energy work is as personal as breath.

In Relationship With Your Energy

When you can meet your energy with care, when you can give it shape, direction, and a safe container, you are no longer at its mercy. You are in relationship with it. You can listen. You can respond. You can choose. And in that relationship, you begin to remember, you are not here to control your feelings. You are here to transform them into something you can live with, and live from.

Eleven

The Four Elements of Transmutation

When you first begin to work with energy, the process can feel abstract, almost impossible to touch. You notice the knot in your chest, the restless hum in your belly, the heat in your throat... and then what?

You can name the sensation. You can even stay with it. But when it's time to guide it into something new, the mind often freezes. How do I take something invisible, something I can feel but not see, and actually shift it? This is where the elements become your allies.

Fire. Water. Earth. Air.

These are not just poetic metaphors. They are the four great movers of the natural world, forces that shape, transform, and guide energy in ways the human body instinctively understands.

Long before we had the language of neuroscience, people worked with these forces to help the body remember how to shift. We built fires to clear space. We bathed in rivers to cleanse grief. We pressed our hands into the soil to ground and steady. We stood in open air to clear the mind.

When you work with the elements in transmutation, you're not "pretending" something is happening, you're giving your nervous system a concrete, sensory anchor. Something you can see, hear, touch, and feel that mirrors the movement you want inside. Ritual creates rhythm, rhythm creates safety and safety is what makes change possible.

The Compass Lives in the Body

In the middle of a real charge, heart racing, hands trembling, thoughts crowding, you won't have time to pull out a notebook and decide which element is "right." You'll need to move quickly, intuitively, without second-guessing. That's where the Elemental Compass comes in.

Choosing your element starts with listening to the language of the energy itself. When you were first learning to notice activation, you practiced turning away from the story ("They're ignoring me again") and toward sensation ("My chest feels tight"). The same applies here, but now, you're feeling for tone, temperature, and movement. Energy speaks through qualities:

Hot — urgent, rising, fiery, demanding to move now

Heavy — dense, sluggish, weighted, lingering

Big — too much at once, flooding, scattered in many directions

Busy — mental noise, swirling thoughts, words jammed at the throat

Each of these qualities responds beautifully to one of the elemental pathways:

Hot → Fire

Heavy → Water

Big → Earth

Busy → Air

When you're in a charge, pause for just a breath and ask: Hot? Heavy? Big? Busy? The word that fits best will point you toward the element that can meet and move that energy.

Fire – Transformation Through Release and Change

Fire is the element of alchemy. It takes what is dense, raw, or heavy and changes it at the most fundamental level. In nature, fire clears forests to make way for new growth. In the body, it burns away what no longer serves and leaves warmth, clarity, and space.

Fire is for the energy that feels hot, urgent, pent-up, the kind that demands to move. Anger, righteous frustration, unspoken truth pressing at the edges of your throat, these are all fuels for fire.

The Vow: "May this fire transform all that is heavy into light, all that is tangled into clarity. I release with care and return to my center."

What it feels like now is raw, charged, restless, volatile. What it can become is focused warmth, clarity, illumination, a steady flame you can work by, not a wildfire that consumes everything.

Full Ritual: Light a candle or safe flame. Write down the feeling, thought, or situation. Speak the vow aloud, then burn the paper. As ash cools, imagine the energy in your body cooling to a steady ember. (Use caution and safe fire practices when burning paper, if you do not trust that you can do this safely you can blow the candle out and bury the paper in the ground or leave it in a safe space like a drawer, keepsake box, or your altar.)

In-the-Moment Version: Inhale gently, drawing the heat down into your belly. Hold for two counts. Exhale slowly, picturing the heat cooling into a steady ember. Whisper: "I choose clarity over combustion."

Everyday Practice: When emotions feel sharp or consuming, I sometimes light a candle with the simple intention of giving the energy somewhere to go. As the flame flickers, I imagine the fire transforming the intensity into warmth, courage, or clarity. When I blow the candle out, I release the remnants with the smoke.

Water – Cleansing, Flow, Softening

Water is the element of release through flow. It teaches that nothing has to be forced, movement comes when we allow it. Water softens what is rigid and carries away what is ready to leave. Water is for the energy that feels heavy, stagnant, or stuck, grief that pools, disappointment that lingers, weariness too thick to shake.

The Vow: "I let this energy flow where it needs to go. May it cleanse, soften, and return me to peace."

What it feels like now is dense, unmoving, clouded. What it can become is clear, adaptable, able to move onward without clinging.

Full Ritual: Place your hands in fresh water and speak the vow. Imagine the heaviness flowing into the water, where it is cleansed. Pour the water into the earth or a drain to symbolize release.

In-the-Moment Version: One palm over your chest, one over your belly. Inhale, imagining a cool stream flowing through you. Exhale, sending the heaviness down into the earth. Whisper: "I let this flow where it needs to go."

Everyday Practice: Sometimes I take a full-body cleanse in the form of a shower, holding the intention of carrying the energy into a flow state. As the water runs over me, I imagine it softening what is rigid and rinsing away what no longer belongs.

Earth – Grounding, Stability, Containment

Earth is the element of steadiness. Not all energy needs to be moved immediately, some needs to be held, composted, and slowly transformed over time. Earth is for the energy that feels over-whelming, scattered, or too large to process at once.

The Vow: "I return this energy to the ground to be made new. I am steady. I am held." What it feels like now is diffuse, unstable, overwhelming. What it can become is rooted presence, steady containment, transformation at the body's natural pace.

Full Ritual: Stand with bare feet on the ground. Hold a stone or wood in your hands. Speak the vow. Imagine sending the energy down through your feet or the object, trusting the earth to hold it.

In-the-Moment Version: Press feet into the floor, palms into thighs. Imagine roots growing deep into the soil. Inhale steadiness up, exhale charge down. Whisper: "I am steady. I am held."

Everyday Practice: When I feel scattered or anxious, I place both hands on the ground, or press my palms against a tree, and let my body remember weight and steadiness. I imagine my energy flowing down into the earth, where it can be held and contained. Even standing barefoot on the soil for a few breaths can return me to stability.

Air – Clarity, Movement, Lightness

Air is the element of perspective and renewal. It moves swiftly, clearing the space around you so you can breathe again. Air is for the energy that feels mental, swirling thoughts, overthinking, words stuck in your throat.

The Vow: "I let this energy rise and disperse. May it clear my mind and return me to openness." What it feels like now is mental clutter, tightness in temples or jaw. What it can become is mental clarity, open breath, lightness of being.

Full Ritual: Stand in open air or by a window. Take a deep breath in, speak the vow on the exhale. Sweep a feather, incense, or even your hand through your field, imagining it carrying away the clutter.

In-the-Moment Version: Inhale through the nose, lift your shoulders slightly to "gather" the clutter. Exhale sharply through the mouth, imagining it scattering into the breeze. Whisper: "I let this rise and disperse."

Everyday Practice: When my thoughts feel tangled, I step outside and breathe deeply. I imagine the wind moving through me, carrying away what no longer serves, clearing space for new breath. Even opening a window and feeling fresh air on my skin can shift my mind into a lighter, freer state.

When You Can't Feel Anything

Sometimes you won't sense "hot," "heavy," "big," or "busy." Instead, you'll feel nothing. Fog. Flatness. Disconnection.

In that stage, your goal is not to match perfectly, it's to start moving toward sensation again. Pick whichever element feels available. If you're at your desk, open a window (air). In the kitchen, wash your hands (water). Outside, place your feet on the ground (earth). At night, light a candle (fire).

Even if you can't feel the shift right away, your nervous system is noticing. Every small act is a signal that it's safe to return to sensing.

The Elemental Compass Works because it bypasses overthinking by reducing choices to four simple qualities. It offers both full rituals and micro-practices so you can work in any setting.

It builds an intuitive link between sensation and action, so over time, you'll respond without needing to "decide."

Becoming the Living Ritual

Life will not always give you perfect conditions for practice. The Rooted Path is not about waiting for an ideal moment, it's about becoming your own container.

Your body, your breath, your imagination, these are enough. The elements are simply ways of remembering what your body already knows, how to burn, flow, root, and clear.

The more you work with them, the more you'll stop doing ritual and start being ritual. You'll carry fire's focus, water's flow, earth's steadiness, and air's clarity in every breath you take. And in that way, transmutation will no longer be something you step into, it will be the way you live.

In the chapter ahead, you will see how integration makes lasting change possible.

Twelve

Integrate

Transmutation changes your state in the moment. Integration teaches your body that the change can last. Without it, a shift is like a wave that rises and falls, leaving the shoreline unchanged. You might feel lighter for a few breaths, minutes, or even hours, but without anchoring, the old pattern often returns. Integration is what transforms a passing breakthrough into a new baseline.

Think of transmutation as remodeling a room, clearing the clutter, changing the light, opening the windows. The space feels fresh and alive. But if you never move in, hang the art, or live there, the room will slowly revert; dust gathers, boxes return, and the newness fades. Integration is moving in. It's inhabiting the change long enough for your nervous system and your cells to register, This is home now.

Biologically, it's the process of rewiring responses through neuroplasticity, consolidating the memory of the shift not just as an idea but as a felt sense, and reinforcing state-dependent learning so the body can return here more easily next time.

Energetically, it's like anchoring a new current in your field. Spiritually, it's the moment you tell yourself, This is who we are now, even if it's still unfamiliar.

Many people skip integration because it's subtle. It doesn't carry the drama of a release or the rush of an "aha" moment, so it can feel optional. But without it, the old grooves remain stronger than the new ones, and the system slips back into its default.

Integration is what strengthens the path you've just opened. It works best when you seal the shift on three levels, body, mind, and energy.

The Body Learns Through Repetition and Sensation

After you've cooled the fire, let the water flow, rooted into earth, or cleared with air, linger in the new state so your body can memorize it. Adjust your posture to reflect the change, spine stacked, shoulders soft, chest open. Notice the weight of your feet on the ground or the depth of your breath. Give this state a physical signature you can recall later.

If you've released grief through water, for example, stay with the lightness in your chest for a few breaths. The next time grief rises, your body will know where it's headed.

The mind, left to itself, will often return to the old story. Integration interrupts this by consciously offering it a new one.

It might be a vow such as I choose care. I choose no harm. A phrase of gratitude like This moment matters, or a statement of identity, I am steady. I am held. When language is paired with the felt sense of the new state, the neural connection between thought and embodiment strengthens.

Energy Responds to Attention

The moment you shift, your field begins to re-pattern, but it needs time to set. Staying still for just a moment after the shift allows this to happen.

Imagine your energy field filling with the new tone, warm, clear, rooted, open, and sealing at the edges like glaze on pottery, keeping what's inside safe. This step is especially important if you're sensitive to other people's energy, because it keeps your shift from being washed away by the next wave you encounter.

One simple way to integrate is to take a brief pause after transmutation. Breathe slowly and deeply three times. Notice one sensation you like about this state. Name the quality or intention you want to carry forward. Seal it with a small gesture, a hand over your heart, palms together, or a gentle bow.

Integration is even more powerful when you carry it into action. If you've turned anger into clarity, speak your truth calmly in the conversation you were about to avoid.

If you've shifted overwhelm into groundedness, take one small, clear step forward. If you've softened grief into compassion, send the message you've been holding back. Each time your body experiences success from this new place, it learns to prefer it, and the baseline changes.

Your Nervous System Re-learns

Every time you integrate, you tell your nervous system, We're not just visiting this place, we live here now. Over time, this builds trust. Your system learns that you won't abandon it after a shift, you'll walk it into the new territory and stay with it there. Eventually, integration stops being a conscious step and becomes your default way of closing the loop.

The main missteps are rushing away too quickly before the shift has time to land, overthinking instead of inhabiting the state, and only integrating in private moments instead of in the real-life contexts where you actually need it.

When you integrate, you're not only stabilizing yourself, you're also affecting the collective field. The stability, clarity, and ground-edness you hold will ripple outward, whether others realize it or not.

The next time you shift, whether through a full ritual or a single breath, pause for just thirty seconds longer than you think you need. Feel the new state in your body. Name it in your mind. Hold it in your field. Then take one small action from that place. This is integration, the bridge between who you were and who you are becoming.

Thirteen

Energy Flow and Movement

E nergy is never still. It moves through you in ways you can learn to feel and shape. There comes a moment in the Rooted Path when you realize you're no longer just noticing a feeling, you're moving it.

At first, that movement often comes through structure. The ritual you've learned, the sequence of steps you follow, your hands resting on your body, your breath finding its rhythm, the vow that names both what you're carrying and what you wish it to become. But with time, something shifts.

You begin to sense the current before you've even named it. You can feel where it's stuck and where it's trying to go. You meet it and guide it, not with force, but with a kind of inner listening. And in that moment you understand that shaping energy isn't rare or mystical. It is deeply human. It has been yours all along.

Energy Is Not Abstract

In the Rooted Path, energy is not abstract. It is the living, shifting sum of sensation, emotion, thought, and presence in your body.

When you hold a charge, whether grief, anger, longing, or even a joy so intense it feels like it might break you open, that charge is physical, chemical, electric, and subtle all at once. It may appear as heat rising in your face, a clench in your gut, buzzing under your skin, heaviness in your chest, tightening in your throat, or an urgent need to act.

Sometimes it's quieter, a low hum of restlessness, looping thoughts, or a slight change in your breathing. These are all signs that energy is moving, or trying to.

From Noticing to Movement

Movement does not mean "get rid of it." Energy cannot be destroyed, but it can change state. A charge can shift from something stuck or chaotic into something steady, usable, and aligned. Energy flow is about guiding that change without losing connection to it.

In the early stages of the Path, you learned to notice without judgment. Then you learned to transmute, giving a charge a container and a pathway for change. You learned to integrate, anchoring the shift so it could last.

Now, you begin to bring those skills into real time. You might feel the pulse in your throat in the middle of a meeting, catch the restless hum in your belly while waiting in traffic, or sense contraction in your field as a conversation turns sharp. Instead of ignoring, suppressing, or letting it take over, guide it as it moves.

Why Movement Matters

Energy is meant to move. In the body, blood circulates, breath flows, lymph drains, and electrical impulses travel.

In the subtle body, prana or qi moves through channels, carrying vitality and information. In the nervous system, sympathetic activation readies you for movement, while parasympathetic states restore and settle you.

Movement is nature's language of renewal. When it stalls, we feel stagnant, depleted, or agitated. When it flows, the system resets.

The First Movers: Hands and Breath

Two of the simplest movers are your hands and your breath. Your palms are rich with nerve endings, and many traditions teach that subtle channels begin or end there.

Placing your hands over the area of strongest sensation gives energy somewhere to go. You can imagine your hands listening, not grabbing or forcing.

On an inhale, draw the sensation toward them. On an exhale, guide it into the ground, into water, or into light. Likewise, breath can move energy on its own.

A slow, steady exhale calms the body and makes space for change. An intentional inhale can draw in the qualities you need, grounding, clarity, compassion.

Grounding as You Move

As you move energy, grounding is essential. Without it, the shift can feel disorienting. Grounding may be physical, pressing your feet into the floor, holding a stone, leaning against a wall, placing your hands in cool water. Or it can be sensory, like naming five things you see, listening for the farthest sound you can hear, or tasting something strong like mint or ginger. Grounding keeps you steady while energy changes state.

From Ritual to Real-Time Flow

In the beginning, you may rely on formal rituals, lighting a candle, pouring water, touching the earth, to anchor your attention and signal your body that it's time to shift.

Over time, these gestures become internal. You'll imagine roots growing from your feet as you breathe through tension.

You'll see a river carry heaviness from your chest into the earth, feel a breeze clearing your mind, or picture a flame softening from blaze to ember. The ritual is still there, but it has become portable, stored in your body memory.

Your Energy Field

Your energy extends beyond your skin. The electromagnetic field of your heart radiates several feet in every direction, with the brain's field adding its own signature.

When you are calm and grounded, this field feels open and steady. When you are agitated or depleted, it can feel contracted or jagged, both to you and to those around you.

You have felt this before, walking into a room after an argument and sensing the heaviness, sitting near someone whose calm slows your own breath, or being in a crowd where excitement vibrates in the air. Energy movement is not only internal, it is relational.

Distance and Connection

That relationship extends beyond physical distance. Many traditions speak of energy traveling across space through prayer, intention, or shared focus. You may have felt warmth simply by thinking of someone with love. If you choose to work with energy this way, do it with respect. Offer it like an open hand, not a push, a candle placed in the dark, not a pull toward the light.

Energy flow is for more than practice sessions. It belongs in your everyday life. In a conversation, you might feel your chest tighten and breathe the tension down into your feet. While washing dishes, irritation might rise and you let the water carry it from your hands into the sink. Walking outside, you might sense mental static and let the breeze take it away. The more often you do this, the more fluent you become.

Children do this naturally, shaking, crying, laughing, running, stomping, curling up until they feel safe again. Adults are often taught to override these instincts. The Rooted Path invites you back to them, not as regression, but as restoration. You are not learning a trick, you are remembering a language.

A Living Skill

Over time, energy flow becomes second nature. You feel a charge, you ground, you move it, you let it shift. You learn when to guide gently, when to let it run its course, and when to hold it longer so it can transform in its own time. You discover that release doesn't always mean letting go entirely, sometimes it means letting the energy become something new within you.

That is the quiet magic of this work, moving energy is not about escaping what you feel. It is about staying with it long enough for it to become something you can live from.

Fourteen

Embody

Over time, The Rooted Path is no longer just something you do, it becomes something you are. In the beginning, the steps feel deliberate. You have to remember them, pausing to think.

Notice. Contain. Transmute. Integrate.

You move through them with care, like learning the steps to a dance. But one day, without realizing when it happened, you notice you're not thinking about the steps anymore. You're simply moving in them.

Your body responds before your mind catches up. Your breath deepens without being told. Your shoulders drop without conscious command. You don't just remember the path, you *are* the path. This is embodiment.

What Embodiment Really Means

To embody a practice is to let it sink so deeply into your nervous system, your energy body, and your lived rhythms that it becomes part of your baseline. It is no longer something you reach for only when you remember, but the ground you walk on without thought.

Embodiment is not perfection. It doesn't mean you never get triggered, never lose your center, or never feel the spike of a charge again. It means that when you do, your return to center is instinctive.

Your body knows the way back even when your mind feels lost. It's the difference between knowing about swimming and actually being able to float when you fall into the water, between memorizing a recipe and being able to cook by feel, between studying a language and one day realizing you are dreaming in it. The Rooted Path was never meant to be memorized or forced, it was meant to be lived.

Why This Step Matters

This step matters because the first three steps (Activate, Transmute, and Integrate) give you the tools to meet, shift, and anchor energy. Without embodiment, those tools remain optional. You have to remember to pick them up.

Embodiment turns those tools into reflexes. It's what allows you to stay rooted even when you're too tired, too busy, or too caught off guard to think your way through a process.

When you've embodied the Rooted Path, your nervous system trusts that you can hold a charge without breaking. Your energy body knows how to move without you pushing. Your choices come from presence rather than panic. This is what transforms the Rooted Path from a practice you do into a way you live.

The Body Learns by Doing

You cannot think your way into embodiment. The body learns by experience, through repetition, sensation, and emotional imprint.

Every time you walk the Rooted Path from start to finish, you're creating new neural pathways. You're teaching your brain, "When a charge comes, this is how we respond now." You're wiring safety into your survival system.

Somatic therapists often say, The body learns what the body lives. If you want the Rooted Path to be second nature, you have to live it enough times that it becomes the body's preferred route.

Signs You're Beginning to Embody the Path

Embodiment doesn't arrive all at once. It seeps in through repetition and attention. You'll know it's happening when you catch activation sooner, noticing the shift in your chest or the buzz in your belly before you've spiraled into reaction, or when your return to calm is faster, taking minutes instead of hours or days.

Your rituals begin to feel less like tools and more like habits. You light the candle, hold the stone, breathe the vow, not because you think you should, but because it's simply how you move through the world now.

You begin to trust yourself in the middle of the storm, knowing you may still feel fear or anger but also knowing you won't abandon yourself there. Others will feel it too. Your steadiness starts to ripple outward, softening conversations and calming rooms without you having to say a word.

Living the Path in Real Time

Living the Path in real time means you no longer have to step away from life to practice it, you practice it in the middle of life.

In a meeting where tension rises, your breath slows on its own. In an argument, your voice stays even while your heart races.

In the grocery store line, you feel frustration spike and, without thinking, you root your feet and let the heat in your body drop into the ground. It's not that you never feel the charge, it's that you meet it with familiarity.

Energy Memory and Muscle Memory

Your nervous system and energy body both carry memory. Just as a musician's fingers find the right chord without conscious thought, your energy system learns the movement of the Path.

This memory is stored in neural pathways, in the vagus nerve that connects brain and body states, in subtle muscle memory, and in the energetic imprint of calm and clarity you've cultivated.

Over time, these layers work together so that when a charge comes, you no longer spiral into old patterns, your whole system leans toward steadiness.

Embodiment and the Field

When you embody the Rooted Path, your personal field changes. The steadiness you've cultivated radiates outward, influencing not just your own state but the collective spaces you move through.

This isn't about controlling others, it's about resonance. Calm has a frequency, and when your field carries it, others can feel it. They may not know why they feel safer around you, but they will.

Just as your field can influence others, theirs can influence you. Embodiment doesn't make you immune to collective energy, but it makes you more resilient within it.

Practices for Deepening Embodiment

To deepen embodiment, you can repeat the Path in varied states, when calm, mildly stressed, and deeply triggered, so your system knows it works in all conditions.

Layer it into daily life, bringing micro-moments of the Path into ordinary actions. Breathing as you stir tea, rooting your feet during a conversation, sending energy down into the ground as you wash your hands.

Create sensory anchors, a scent, a stone, a song, so that over time, these cues automatically return you to steadiness. Reflect on your progress. Notice the moments when the Path happens without effort and write them down, so you can see embodiment forming.

The Difference Between Integration and Embodiment

It's helpful to remember the difference between integration and embodiment. Integration is about anchoring a single shift so it lasts in your system.

Embodiment is about stacking those shifts until they become your foundation. If integration is planting one seed, embodiment is the forest that grows when you keep planting and tending over time.

When Embodiment Feels Far Away

If embodiment feels far away, there's no need to chase it. You don't have to aim at embodiment, you just have to keep walking the Path. Every time you do, you teach your body something new. One day, you'll notice you've stayed present through something that would have undone you before, and you'll realize embodiment has quietly arrived.

– A Story from the Path –
A friend used to think she had no self-control.
Any time she felt criticized, she'd lash out or shut down completely.

When she began the Rooted Path, she practiced the steps in small moments.

A brief pause before sending a text, a grounding breath before answering a question.

Months later, she told me about a family dinner where an old pattern was triggered.

She felt the heat in her chest, the tightness in her jaw, and without thinking she took a slow breath, placed her hands on her thighs under the table, and let the heat run into the ground.

Her family kept talking. She stayed steady. No one else even noticed, but she did.

"That was the first time I realized I am the Path now," she said. "I didn't have to remember it. I was it."

Embodiment as Belonging to Yourself

At its heart, embodiment is about belonging — to your body, your breath, your energy, your choices. It means you no longer feel like a stranger to yourself in moments of intensity. You know your own language. You trust your own ground. You belong to yourself, even in the storm.

The Rooted Path doesn't end with embodiment, because embodiment is not a finish line. It is the beginning of living in a different rhythm.

You'll still learn. You'll still be surprised. You'll still be human. But you'll be human with roots and a way home. A human whose body remembers how to return, no matter how far the wind blows you, and that changes everything.

Fifteen

The Roots Beneath the Path

The Rooted Path is not a brand-new structure built from nothing. It's something ancient, remembered in pieces across traditions, and shaped by necessity in my own life. It did not arrive as a neat formula. It revealed itself slowly, through breath and breaking. In trembling hands that learned to steady. Through storms that stripped my branches bare and exposed my roots beneath.

Across cultures and centuries, people have spoken of the current that moves through us. In Ayurveda, it is prana, the vital life force that animates breath, digestion and heartbeat. When we live out of rhythm with nature, truth, or our own inner knowing, prana becomes disturbed. The channels (nadis) constrict, and vitality wanes. But when prana flows freely, balance returns. Health is not simply the absence of disease. It is also the presence of deep vitality.

In Traditional Chinese Medicine, this same living current is called qi. Qi flows through meridians, nourishing every organ and tissue. When it is blocked by tension, repression, or trauma — imbalance follows. Acupuncture, herbs, movement, and breath are all ways to restore its flow.

These systems all agree that energy is not separate from the body, it is the body. Healing is not about repair from the outside. It's about loosening the inner soil so the roots can drink again.

Modern Science & Ancient Truth

Neuroscience now echoes what ancient wisdom has long carried. Polyvegal theory shows how the nervous system shifts between safety and survival in response to subtle cues long before the mind tells a story.

This is why some people shut down after conflict while others erupt. Why one person freezes in the presence of fear and another floods with anger. The nervous system is not failing, it is adapting, always scanning, always adjusting to keep us alive.

Somatic therapies build on this, asking us to feel emotions in the body instead of overriding them. Notice the heat, the trembling, the urge to move.

Mindfulness and breathwork teach us to meet what is here without piling on more. Trauma-informed care reminds us that safety must come before pressure. Each approach is a doorway into the same truth. The body already knows how to move energy, if we stop interrupting it.

Where the Roots Took Hold

These ideas helped me at different times, but when my body was in full reaction, I couldn't remember which practice to reach for. I didn't need a checklist. I needed something I could do with shaking hands and a racing pulse.

That's when the Rooted Path began to form. Not as a polished method, but as a way to stay in the living middle, not clinging to control, not surrendering to chaos, but staying with the energy until it shifted.

Something You Can Hold in the Storm

The Rooted Path can be carried into a therapy session or a sacred ceremony. It can be carried into the kitchen during an argument, into the grocery store when your chest tightens in a crowd, or the back seat of a car when your child is melting down.

It isn't a replacement for your other practices. It's the ground they grow from, the rich, dark soil that holds them steady. It gathers what is most useful from science and somatics. It honors the energetic and spiritual. It gives you something simple enough to carry even in the storm.

A Living Path

This is not about "calming down." It's about reshaping your baseline. With each return to the Path, you teach your nervous system a new rhythm. Over time, the new pattern takes root.

I do not offer this as a theory or as someone who has "arrived." I offer it as someone who couldn't find a map simple enough to follow when I was breaking. So I began drawing one in the dirt with my own hands. If you resonate with this, it's not because I'm telling you something new, it's because something in you already knew. You are not learning from me, you are remembering with me.

We've always known how to transmute energy. We've always known that pain can soften into power. That grief can become love. That anger can become clarity. The Rooted Path doesn't invent this knowing. It only gives it a name, a rhythm. A place to return, again and again, whenever the winds rise.

Sixteen

Why It's Harder for Some

Not everyone meets the Rooted Path on level ground. Some arrive at its edge after years of climbing. Climbing out of old wounds, through exhaustion, through a terrain that has taught them that safety is rare and calm is suspicious, and this matters.

When you hear about a practice that asks you to pause, to stay, to feel, you might think... "I've tried that before, and it didn't work for me." Or worse, "It worked for other people, but not for me. Something must be wrong with me."

The truth? It's not that something is wrong with you. It's that you've been living in conditions that make this work more challenging. That's exactly why it can also be more important.

The Weight You Carry into the Path

Every person begins here with a unique map, not just of their mind, but of their nervous system, their energy body, and their lived history. Some maps are wide open, with clear pathways between feeling and regulation. Others are tangled with detours, blockages, and dead ends, because the road to safety has been disrupted so many times.

When you've lived through chronic stress, trauma, illness, oppression, neglect, or relentless uncertainty, your baseline is not the same as someone who has known mostly steady ground. Your nervous system's "starting point" may be closer to hypervigilance or shutdown. Your energy field may feel contracted, frayed, or thin. Your body may not trust that pausing is safe.

None of this is a personal failing. It's a reflection of what you've survived.

Why the Path Feels Harder

There are a few common reasons some people find the Rooted Path more challenging at first. One of those reasons may be that your nervous system has been on high alert for years. If you've lived in survival mode, your body's neuroception (the unconscious scanning for safety or danger) may be tuned to pick up threat everywhere. The moment you feel a charge, your system might flood with adrenaline, tighten your muscles, and prepare you to fight, flee, or freeze. Pausing in that state feels unnatural, even unsafe.

For others, the challenge isn't over-activation, it's disconnection. Long-term stress or trauma can lead to a "frozen" state where sensation is muted. This protective fog keeps you from feeling the extremes, but it also makes it harder to notice the subtler shifts that the Rooted Path begins with. You might not even be sure you're "doing it right" because you can't sense much at first.

Another reason could be that your energy body is carrying more than just yours. Some people are naturally more empathic, more attuned to the emotional tone of a room, a relationship, or even the collective mood. If you've been absorbing others' emotions for years, it can be difficult to tell which charges are yours and which are "borrowed." The Rooted Path requires discernment, and that discernment takes time to build when your system is used to blending.

Old patterns are deeply rooted. The ways you've learned to survive, people-pleasing, over-explaining, shutting down, or lashing out may be decades old. Your brain and body have practiced them so well they run automatically. The Rooted Path interrupts those patterns, but at first the old grooves will feel more familiar, more "right," than the new way.

It could also be that you're working against cultural currents. In many cultures, slowing down, feeling, and attending to your inner life is treated as weakness, self-indulgence, or a waste of time. The world rewards speed, productivity, and external control. Choosing the Rooted Path can feel like swimming upstream against the current of "just get over it" or "keep it together."

Why This Isn't a Reason to Give Up

It's easy to read all of this and think, "well, that explains why it's so hard for me. Maybe I should just stop trying". Here's the quiet truth, the very conditions that make this work harder for you also make it more essential.

If your nervous system has been in overdrive for years, every small moment of rootedness is medicine. If you've been in the fog, every flicker of sensation is a sign that your system is thawing. If you've been carrying what isn't yours, every act of discernment strengthens your boundaries. If your old patterns are deeply etched, every time you choose differently, you're carving a new path. If you're moving against the cultural current, every pause you take is an act of reclamation.

Meeting Yourself Where You Are

The Rooted Path is not a race, and it's not a pass/fail test. The point is not to get to the "end" as quickly as possible. The point is to build roots strong enough to hold you, no matter how long it takes for them to grow. If you know the path will be harder for you, that's not a prediction of failure. It's an invitation to approach the work with even more compassion, patience, and flexibility.

Start Smaller Than You Think You Need To

Instead of trying to work with a massive charge right away, choose something mild, an everyday irritation, a small moment of disappointment, a gentle wave of restlessness. Success here builds trust and capacity.

Grounding isn't an optional add-on. If your system is jumpy or frozen, grounding is the doorway in. You might spend days or weeks focusing on grounding alone before moving into full transmutation.

If sensation feels distant, trust that noticing anything is progress, the weight of your hands, the sound in the room, the rhythm of your breath. Over time, those small openings become wider.

When internal sensing is faint or chaotic, external ritual gives you something tangible to hold. The candle, the stone, the breath, the words, these are handholds until your body can feel the shift more directly.

The Hidden Advantage of a Hard Beginning

It might feel unfair to start here with more to carry. But there's a quiet advantage to learning the Rooted Path from a harder place.

You will become exquisitely skilled at reading your own system and honoring its pace.

Those who have had to earn every inch of safety tend to be more precise, more patient, and more attuned to subtle shifts, in themselves and in others. If you stay with the practice, you may find that what once felt like a disadvantage becomes one of your greatest strengths.

– A Story from the Path –

I once worked with someone who came to the Rooted Path after years of chronic illness, burnout, and trauma.
In her words, "I'm not sure I even have feelings anymore, I just have symptoms."
We started with nothing more than placing her feet on the ground for thirty seconds each morning. That was it. No analysis, no deep dives, no big emotional releases.
For weeks, she felt nothing, just the pressure of her feet on the floor.
But one day, she noticed the faintest warmth moving up her calves. Weeks later, she felt a flutter of irritation during a phone call and stayed with it instead of swallowing it down.
It took months before she could work through the full sequence of the Rooted Path with a strong charge. But when she did, she told me, "If I had tried to force it in the beginning, I would have quit.
Starting small didn't just help, it made it possible."

If this work feels harder for you, you are not late, slow, or failing. You are moving at the exact pace your system can handle, and that is the pace that will let it last.

The Rooted Path is about becoming deeply rooted in yourself. Roots don't grow overnight. They reach down in the dark, slowly, deliberately, until they find the water and stability they need. If you give them time, they will hold you.

Seventeen

Troubleshooting The Rooted Path

The Rooted Path is simple, but simple doesn't mean easy. Even with clear steps, it's natural to hit points where the practice feels clunky, flat, or frustrating. This chapter is your troubleshooting guide, not to make you "perfect" at the Path, but to help you see where you might be unintentionally tripping yourself and how to step back into flow.

Mistakes here aren't failures, they're messages. Each one shows you exactly where your system needs more attention, more support, or a different approach. Sometimes, it isn't even a mistake at all, it's that the Path is working in quieter, subtler ways than you expect. Either way, if you find yourself thinking "It's not working", this chapter is here to walk with you.

Mistake 1: Skipping the Pause

When activation hits, it's tempting to rush into fixing, deep breathing, self-talk, distraction. Or to rush into reacting, speaking, moving, deciding before you've even felt the first full wave.

But if you skip the pause, you skip the meeting point between you and your energy. Without that meeting, you're not transmuting, you're just shifting the surface without touching the root.

How to Troubleshoot:

Even one breath of pause matters. Make it intentional. Anchor to sensation first, not story. My chest is tight. My palms are warm. My stomach feels hollow. Remind yourself, "This is the moment that matters."

Mistake 2: Starting Too Big

Many try to begin with the most overwhelming, unresolved charge in their life. "If I can do it with this, I can do it with anything," they think. But starting too big can flood you, leaving you exhausted, discouraged, or more reactive.

How to Troubleshoot:

Scale way down. Begin with mild irritation or a small worry. Practice on everyday charges until it feels natural. Build capacity like building muscle. Light weight first, more over time.

Mistake 3: Trying to "Get Rid" of the Energy

If your focus is to make this go away, you're still in control mode. This keeps your system braced. Energy doesn't respond well to being erased, but it will respond to being guided.

How to Troubleshoot:

Change your inner language from stop to shift. Ask, "what do I want this energy to become?" clarity, compassion, steadiness. Remember, transmutation changes form, not existence.

Mistake 4: Overthinking the Steps

The Rooted Path has a sequence, but it isn't a rigid script. If you're analyzing each move, you've slipped back into your head.

How to Troubleshoot:
If you're narrating instead of feeling, stop and place a hand on your body. Improvise. The order matters less than your presence. Treat the steps as a compass, not a cage.

Mistake 5: Forgetting to Ground

Without grounding, energy work can leave you spacey, dizzy, or raw.
How to Troubleshoot:
Ground first, feet on the floor, breath in your chest. Ground during if the charge feels too big. Ground afterwards to signal completion. Lean into a wall, place your hands on thighs, name five things you see.

Mistake 6: Rushing Integration

Once energy shifts, it's tempting to move on. But if you don't give your system time to feel the new state, the old one can sneak back.
How to Troubleshoot:
When you feel a shift, stay with it at least 30 seconds. Seal the moment with a gesture or vow. Think of integration like cooling bread: let it set before you slice.

Mistake 7: Expecting Big Fireworks Every Time

Some practices feel subtle, even unremarkable. That doesn't mean nothing happened. Energy shifts quietly as often as it does dramatically.
How to Troubleshoot:
Trust small signs, softer shoulders, steadier breath, clearer gaze. Keep a simple log to notice patterns. Release the idea that only "big" counts.

Mistake 8: Only Practicing in Crisis

If you only practice during major surges, it will always feel uphill.
How to Troubleshoot:
Practice daily in mild or neutral moments. Build muscle memory so the Path is easier when it's needed most.

Mistake 9: Ignoring Capacity

Sometimes the skillful choice is not to practice. If you're depleted, sick, or overwhelmed, forcing the process can backfire.
How to Troubleshoot:
Listen for your body's "no." If you get it, focus on rest or gentle grounding instead. Trust that pausing is part of rooting.

Mistake 10: Treating the Path as a Mechanical Tool

The Path is not just steps, it's a relationship with your energy.
How to Troubleshoot:
Speak to yourself like a friend. Remember energy is not an enemy, it's you. Let your way of walking evolve as you evolve.

When the Path Seems Not to Work

Even with all this, there will be days when you walk the Path and... nothing. No shift, no relief, no clarity. The charge stays, or even grows. This is when people often think, "maybe this isn't for me."

But there's no such thing as "it didn't work." There's only "it didn't work how I expected." Often, those moments are part of the work itself.

Reason 1: You're in the Middle of a Big Wave

Some charges are storms that have built for years. One round of practice won't dissolve them, and that's not failure. Work gently, one thread at a time. Sometimes the "win" is simply not making the knot tighter.

Reason 2: Your System Is Over Capacity

If you're depleted, your system may not have the reserves to shift energy. Focus on rest first. Use grounding-only practices. Return when your baseline energy is higher.

Reason 3: Fighting Instead of Meeting

If your agenda is to stop now, your system hears resistance. Shift your inner tone from combat to curiosity. Remember, you're inviting change, not erasing existence.

Reason 4: It's Not Just Your Energy

Sometimes you're resonating with others, family, coworkers, the collective. Ask, what's mine? What's not mine? Release what isn't yours with a vow or boundary.

Reason 5: Not Enough Practice Yet

The Path is a skill, not a trick. Like muscle memory, it takes repetition. Practice daily in small doses. Value consistency over intensity.

Reason 6: The Shift Is Subtle

Sometimes the change is quieter than your expectations. Scan for small signs. Learn to value whispers as much as shouts.

Reason 7: It's About Integration, Not Relief

Sometimes practice is laying groundwork for next time. Notice if the charge feels less consuming. Credit yourself for showing up, that act itself rewires the pattern.

Reason 8: Old Layers Are Surfacing

Instead of settling, sometimes more rises up. This isn't regression, it's release. Work one layer at a time. Ground and contain. Remind yourself, this is what healing looks like sometimes.

When to Take a Break

The Rooted Path is meant to support, not punish. If practice leaves you consistently worse, pause and seek support, from therapy, energy work, or trusted companions. Pausing is not failure. It's one of the most rooted choices you can make.

– A Story from the Path –

One man I worked with could recite every step perfectly.
But when we practiced, he stayed tense.
He was skipping the pause without realizing it, moving straight from activation to shifting.
Once he slowed down to actually feel the first sensations, the practice began to work.
It wasn't about more effort, it was about less rushing.

– Another Story from the Path –

A woman told me, "I tried it three times.
Nothing happened."
But when I pointed out her breath deepened during practice, she dismissed it.
"That's just my breath."
What she didn't realize is that her breath was the shift.

Once she began noticing and trusting the subtle changes, the Path became alive for her.

When the Path feels stuck, check your expectations, check your capacity and check your consistency. The measure of success isn't dramatic results every time. It's whether you stay in relationship with your energy, even when it's stubborn. Even when nothing seems to move, you are still rooting. And that, more than any immediate relief, is the heart of the Path.

Eighteen

Signs of Progress

When you first begin walking the Rooted Path, progress can feel slippery. Some days, the change is obvious. You catch yourself before the spiral, you breathe, choose differently. Other days, you wonder if anything is shifting at all.

The truth is, growth along the Path often arrives in small, subtle ways before it makes big, dramatic entrances. It's like the first green shoots in spring. They're easy to miss if you're only looking for full blossoms.

Recognizing the signs matters. Not only because it keeps you from giving up too soon, but because noticing progress is progress. When you can see your own shifts, you reinforce them. You give your system proof that this is working so that you keep going.

Notice the Charge Sooner

In the early days, you might only realize you've been hijacked after you've snapped, shut down, or spiraled. The Path teaches you to catch the moment earlier and earlier, sometimes even before the reaction starts.

Why does this matter? Early awareness gives you more choice. You can meet the energy before it takes the wheel.

Instead of realizing two hours later, "I was so anxious in that meeting," you notice the flutter in your chest during the meeting. That single moment of noticing is a turning point.

The Charge Feels Less Overpowering

The same triggers may still appear, but their impact softens. The wave still comes, but it's smaller, or you're standing on steadier ground when it hits.

This means your nervous system is building resilience. The circuits of reactivity are being balanced by circuits of regulation.

Where before you might have gone from "slightly irritated" to "furious" in seconds, now there's a pause, a gap you can breathe into.

You Stay Present Longer

Progress isn't about never being thrown off. It's about how long it takes you to come back. If, in the past, a sharp email would ruin your whole day, now you may find yourself unsettled for an hour, then steady again.

Every time you return faster, you're teaching your body that it can recover, and recovery is the foundation of lasting calm.

Physical Tension Releases More Easily

At first, your body may stay tight long after a charge. Over time, you'll notice that your shoulders drop, your jaw loosens, or your breath deepens much sooner after using the Path.

Physical release is a sign your vagus nerve is activating and your parasympathetic (rest-and-digest) state is returning.

You Can Name Your State Without Judgment

In the beginning, activation often comes with self-criticism. Why am I like this? I should be over this by now. Progress looks like being able to say, "I feel tightness in my chest," without adding the layer of blame.

Judgment keeps the nervous system in threat mode. Neutral naming signals safety, which makes shifting easier.

You Use the Path in the Middle of Life

In the early stages, practice may only feel possible in quiet, controlled moments. Later, you'll notice yourself using the Path while talking to your child, sitting at your desk, or standing in line at the store.

This shows the practice is integrating into your everyday life. It's no longer a "separate" thing, but part of how you move through the world.

You Recover from "Missed Moments" with Kindness

At first, missing a practice opportunity might send you into self-criticism. Later, you can notice, "I reacted just then," and choose to come back without shame.

This is one of the deepest shifts, moving from perfectionism to relationship. The Path is not about getting it right every time. It's about returning, again and again.

You Begin to Sense Energy More Clearly

If you started in fog, you may notice sensations returning, heat, heaviness, buzzing, or lightness in specific parts of the body. If you already felt sensations strongly, you may notice more nuance, the difference between sharp, restless heat and steady, grounded warmth. Clarity in sensation gives you more precision in choosing how to work with it.

You feel more in charge of your choices. This doesn't mean you control what rises. It means you control how you meet it. You realize, I don't have to send that message right now. I can choose another tone. I can walk away. This is the heart of the Rooted Path: restoring your power to choose without abandoning yourself.

Others Notice the Difference

Sometimes the first signs of change come from outside you, a friend saying, "You seem calmer lately," or a coworker noting, "You handled that better than most people would have." External reflection can help you see progress you might have missed in yourself.

Over time, you stop fearing certain feelings. You realize you can hold grief without drowning, anger without burning, joy without losing your footing. This expanded capacity is what allows deeper healing. You no longer need to avoid your own aliveness.

You Carry the Elements in Your Body Memory

At first, you may need the full ritual, the candle, the water, the stone, the open window. Later, you can shift energy with a breath and a single image.

This is a sign of mastery, the Path has moved from external structure to internal fluency. You may notice that time seems to "slow" in charged moments. There's more room between what happens and what you do next.

That space is where transformation lives. Without it, you're in reaction. With it, you're in creation.

In the beginning, you might want to "fix" the charge right away. Later, you can breathe with it, listening until it shifts in its own time.

This patience deepens your relationship with your energy, and teaches your system it doesn't need to fear activation. You can hold energy without needing to discharge it immediately.

You Begin to Live From the Rooted State

The deepest sign of progress isn't what happens during practice, it's who you are outside of it. You notice more ease in your body, more clarity in your choices, more kindness toward yourself. You're not just using the Path; you are the Path.

– A Story from the Path –

A young man started practicing with intense self-doubt.
He told me, "I never know if I'm doing it right."
A few months later, he was in a tense work meeting.
His chest tightened, his thoughts raced.
Without anyone noticing, he placed his feet flat on the floor,
exhaled slowly, and let the tightness sink into the ground.
Later, he told me, "I don't know if it worked."
I asked, "Did you explode? Did you shut down?"
He smiled. "No. I just stayed." That is the work. That's the sign.

Your Progress Is Yours

Your signs of progress might not look like anyone else's. For some, the biggest shift is going from daily panic attacks to one a month. For others, it's catching anger before it hits their voice. For some, it's feeling anything after years of numbness.

The point isn't to meet someone else's measure, it's to notice your own. Keep a small record. Write down even the tiniest signs:

"I noticed my breath." "I paused before answering.""I felt my feet."
Over time, these small notes will tell the story of your becoming.

Part III – Living the Rooted Path

Before You Continue

The Rooted Path and the practices in this book are tools for personal growth, self-awareness, and emotional regulation. They are not a replacement for medical, psychological, or therapeutic advice, diagnosis, or treatment.

I am not a medical professional. Nothing here should be taken as medical guidance. If you are experiencing persistent physical symptoms, overwhelming emotional distress, or thoughts of harming yourself, please seek help from a qualified healthcare provider or mental health professional.

You are the expert on your own body and life. Take what resonates, leave what doesn't, and adapt every practice to your own needs and capacity. Your safety and steadiness come first. Always.

For Practitioners and Guides

If you are a therapist, coach, healer, or other helping professional, you are welcome to adapt the concepts and practices in this book to support your clients in your own language and style as part of your existing work.

The Rooted Path™ name, framework, and training materials are proprietary and may only be taught or presented as a branded method with the author's written consent. If you feel called to integrate The Rooted Path™ into your professional practice in a formal way, you can train and certify through the practitioner program.

However you choose to use these tools, thank you for the work you do in helping others return to themselves.

Nineteen

Stillness, Letting Go, and Becoming

The Rooted Path is not only about what you do in the storm. It is also about how you return to quiet after the storm has passed. To stay rooted is not to be endlessly bracing for impact, but to find the ground where nothing is demanded of you, where you can simply be.

The Practice of Stillness

Stillness is not the absence of movement. It is the space where movement no longer controls you. In stillness, the nervous system learns it does not always have to anticipate, react, or protect. The body can rest without abandoning alertness. The mind can soften without losing awareness.

For many, stillness can feel intimidating at first. Silence stirs what has been buried. The mind rushes in with lists and worries. The body fidgets as if it has forgotten how to be still. But the point of stillness is not to "empty" yourself, it is to remember that you already carry enough.

Stillness can be a pause between breaths, the moment before you answer, the three seconds you rest your hand on your chest before moving on. The more often you allow yourself to visit this place, the more your body remembers it is safe to return.

Meditation as Remembering

Meditation is often taught as a discipline, a way to control thoughts or strive toward enlightenment. On the Rooted Path, it is something quieter, a way of remembering. You are not trying to transcend yourself, but to return to yourself.

Meditation can be as simple as noticing sensation. The coolness of air as you breathe in. The warmth of air as you breathe out. The rise and fall of your chest. The hum of your pulse.

Thoughts will come, and that is not a failure. Each time you notice them and return to your breath or body, you are strengthening the root of awareness. It is less about "clearing the mind" and more about anchoring presence. Over time, this practice makes it easier to sense the small shifts of energy before they spiral into overwhelm.

Meditation is not about achieving stillness. It is about practicing relationship with stillness until it feels familiar, until you trust that you can enter it and return safely.

Letting Go

Every charge, every memory, every grief leaves an imprint. Some imprints hold wisdom. Others weigh you down long after their purpose has passed. Letting go is not about discarding your past or pretending pain never happened. It is about releasing what no longer serves who you are becoming.

On the Rooted Path, letting go is often a subtle shift, not a dramatic release. It might be the unclenching of your jaw after realizing you've been holding it tight all day. It might be writing down words you no longer need to carry and placing the paper in a flame, water, or earth. It might be as simple as saying aloud, "I release this now. I am safe without it."

Release does not erase. It transforms. What once felt like a stone in your chest can become compost for growth. What once felt like a weight on your shoulders can become strength in your spine. Letting go is less about losing something and more about making space for what wants to grow.

The Mask That Knows It's a Mask

Not everything in your life will immediately align with your becoming. Sometimes you'll find yourself wearing something that doesn't quite fit, a job, a role, a habit of survival. It's easy to fear that these things mean you're lost, or that you've betrayed yourself. But there's a difference between being trapped in a mask and wearing a mask knowingly.

A mask becomes dangerous only when you forget it's there. When you confuse it with your true face, you begin to shrink into something smaller than you are. But when you can name it, this is temporary, this is not me, this is what I need to hold for now, then the mask loses its power. It becomes a bridge, not a prison.

You are not the job you endure. You are not the silence you once had to keep. You are not the coping mechanism that helped you survive. You can hold them, use them, even walk with them for a time. But when the day comes, you will set them down — and the light underneath will still be whole, still be yours. Discernment is the practice of remembering that masks are temporary. You are not.

The Tree of Becoming

Stillness and release are not the end of the Path, they are the conditions for growth. When you slow down enough to rest, when you allow what no longer serves you to fall away, the Tree of Becoming grows naturally. Roots deepen. Branches extend. Leaves reach toward the light.

Becoming is not a single moment of change, it is a lifetime of tending. Every time you pause to feel your breath, you are becoming. Every time you let go of a charge instead of clinging to it, you are becoming. Every time you choose presence instead of old reflexes, you are becoming.

This chapter is not here to teach you how to fix yourself, but to remind you that your growth is already underway. Stillness shows you the soil. Letting go clears the stones. Meditation waters the roots. And becoming is the quiet, steady unfolding that follows, the tree that grows not in spite of the storms, but through them.

Twenty

Adapting the Rooted Path Overview

One of the strengths of the Rooted Path is its structure.
Activate. Transmute. Integrate. Embody

Each step is clear, teachable, and repeatable. Though life is not a controlled environment, it's messy and layered. While the steps are the same, the way you walk them will shift depending on where you are, what's happening, and who you're with. This is why adaptation matters.

When you know how to adjust the Path to the moment, it becomes more than a practice you do. It becomes a living skill you carry. It can fit into a grief ritual as easily as it can slip into a thirty-second pause before answering your child's question. It can meet you in the depths of heartbreak or in the middle of a crowded grocery store.

The goal of adaptation is not to dilute the Path or skip steps. It's to learn how each step can flex. Learn how to scale it down when time is short, scale it up when you need depth, and modify it when your environment or state makes the original form impractical.

Why Adaptation Is a Skill in Itself

Some people feel safe practicing the Path only in quiet, private spaces at first. Others feel comfortable trying it mid-conversation but freeze if they can't light a candle or step outside. Adaptation lets you take the heart of the practice with you anywhere, without losing its effectiveness.

Think of it like learning a language. In class, you might form perfect sentences. But in real life, when you're hungry and tired and trying to order food in a busy café, you use the short version. The meaning is the same but the delivery is different. The more fluent you become in the Path, the more you can "speak" it in any setting.

The Four Dimensions of Adaptation

These four factors will influence how you adjust the steps.

Time – How much space do you have before you need to act or respond?

Environment – Are you in a private, supportive space, or a public, high-pressure one?

Intensity – How strong is the charge? Is it a mild discomfort or a wave that threatens to knock you down?

Capacity – Where are you today? Are you rested and resourced, or already at your limit?

Scaling the Path

Full Form: This is the complete practice. All steps, deliberate pacing, full sensory engagement. This might be a half-hour at home, with your journal, an element ritual, and time to integrate deeply.

Mid-Form: You move through all steps, but more quickly. You might have five minutes in your car before going into a meeting. You breathe, name the charge, use a mental version of your chosen element, and anchor with a vow or grounding gesture.

Micro-Form: This is the "emergency shorthand." You condense the steps into seconds: notice, choose one breath, recall the element in your mind's eye, shift just enough to steady yourself until you can practice more fully later.

When the Charge Is Too Big

Sometimes the energy is more than you can meet in the moment, especially with fresh grief, trauma activation, or layered stress. Adaptation here means focusing on containment before transformation.

You might skip a full transmutation ritual and instead ground into earth by pressing your feet firmly down. Hold a protective object in your hand. Speak a single phrase. "I will meet this later. I am safe enough right now."

Containment is not avoidance. It's an intentional pause, holding the energy safely until you have the space and support to process it.

When the Environment Won't Allow Privacy

You may not be able to close your eyes, speak a vow aloud, or light incense in a boardroom, classroom, or airplane. Adaptation here means learning the invisible Path.

Instead of a physical candle (fire), imagine a steady ember in your core. Instead of water in your hands, visualize a cool stream running down your spine. Instead of standing barefoot on the ground, imagine roots from your feet sinking deep into the floor.

Instead of wind at your face, picture a fresh breeze clearing your chest.

The element still works because your body responds to imagery almost as strongly as it does to direct sensation.

When You Have Seconds

The smallest adaptation is the single breath. Inhale to notice. Exhale to shift. That's it. It's not the whole practice but it's enough to interrupt the automatic reaction and give you a foothold.

Some people worry that shortening the Path makes it weaker. In truth, the nervous system responds to small cues as powerfully as large ones, especially when they are repeated over time.

A quick micro-practice in the moment, followed by a deeper session later, can be even more effective than trying to "push through" with the full form when you're not able to be present for it.

Making It Yours

Adaptation isn't about memorizing every possible variation. It's about knowing what works for you. Some people anchor best with movement; others with imagery; others with sound or touch. The more you practice in different contexts, the more you discover your own reliable entry points.

Life will never wait for the "perfect" moment to challenge you. The car alarm will go off while you're meditating. The phone will ring in the middle of your grounding ritual. You will be asked to respond before you're ready. Adaptation is what allows you to stay rooted anyway.

– A Story from the Path –

A nurse I worked with practiced the full Path at home and felt confident until she tried it during a high-stress shift in the ER.

"There was no way I could stop and go through all the steps," she told me. "I thought I failed."

We built her a micro-form:

Feet pressed into the floor (Activate + Ground).

One deep exhale (Transmute).

Hand briefly over her heart (Integrate).

Return to task.

"It takes me about six seconds," she said later. "And it changes everything."

From Adapting to Embodying

Adaptation is a bridge that connects the structured learning of the Path to the intuitive living of the Path. The more you adapt, the more fluent you become, until the adjustments aren't something you think about they're something you are.

The chapters ahead will take this overview and apply it to specific contexts, grief, attraction, anxiety, parenting, work, health, creativity, and more, so you can see exactly how to let the Path bend without breaking in the moments that matter most. The goal isn't to practice perfectly, it's to keep walking no matter where you are no matter what rises.

Twenty One

The Missing Half of
Healing

M odern medicine in the United States is brilliant at emergen-
cies. If you have a heart attack, need surgery, or are fighting
a severe infection, the system moves fast and can save your life.

But what happens after that? What happens when the infection
is gone, but the treatment has stripped your gut of its balance?
When the scans are "clear," but your hormones are still erratic and
your sleep is broken? When the pain has been "managed," but the
inflammation quietly keeps burning underneath?

The truth is, for many people, medical care stops the moment
the immediate danger is over. The rest... the rebuilding, the recal-
ibration, the return to full vitality, is left up to the patient. And in
a system that rarely looks beyond its own specialty lens, that second half of healing is often ignored entirely.

The Strengths and Limits of the Current Model

I don't write this to attack the medical field. It has saved count-
less lives, and I would never want to live without it. But it was

built for crisis, not for the slow work of restoring an entire human system.

It shines at stopping disease in its tracks, repairing acute injuries, managing life-threatening infections, and performing complex surgeries

It struggles at multi-system, long-term conditions (autoimmune, neurodegenerative, post-infection syndromes.) Individual variation is often needed in recovery. It often misses addressing or identifying the root causes for chronic inflammation or fatigue. It doesn't integrate emotional, hormonal, immune, and gut health into one plan.

Patients with complex or chronic issues quickly find themselves being referred from one specialist to another. Gastroenterology for the gut, endocrinology for hormones, psychiatry for anxiety. Without anyone zooming out to see how it all connects, we often miss what lies at the root entirely.

The Real Impact of Missing Backend Support

This is where people like my friend get stuck. She had a severe infection and was told by her doctor, "If you don't take this antibiotic, you could die." She listened and in that moment, it probably saved her life. But the follow-up care ended there.

No one helped her restore her microbiome. No one warned her about possible long-term gut disruption. When problems started, bloating, food sensitivities, digestive swings. The advice was piecemeal, and often contradictory.

She dove into gut health research, learning everything she could about probiotics, prebiotics, and diet. But even with all her knowledge, progress was slow, because one major piece was missing. Her nervous system was still living in a state of high alert. And that made it almost impossible for her body to receive the healing she was working so hard to create.

Why Healing Can't Land in a Stressed Body

The body has priorities. When it believes it's in danger, whether from old trauma, current stress, or constant worry about symptoms, it diverts energy away from digestion, immune repair, and hormone balance.

It doesn't matter how perfect the diet is, how carefully supplements are chosen, or how many protocols are followed, if the nervous system is in fight-or-flight, the gates to deep healing stay partly closed.

For my friend, it wasn't just her old trauma creating this stress load. It was the ongoing fear about her gut health, the frustration of feeling like every food might set her back, and the exhaustion of managing it all without guidance.

This is where The Rooted Path begins, not with another supplement or elimination plan, but with regulation first. Calm the system. Let the body feel safe again. Open the door for healing to walk in.

How The Rooted Path Fills the Gap

I am not a doctor, I don't diagnose or prescribe. What I do is help people reconnect to the part of themselves that can guide healing from the inside out.

Step one is regulation. Gentle nervous system practices that signal safety. Breathing techniques to activate the parasympathetic "rest and digest" state. Mind-body tools to help release the constant state of bracing.

Once you are more calm and open you can begin gentle rebuilding. The body feels safer so that we can now support the terrain, digestion, sleep, immune balance, and steady energy. This is where gut healing steps, dietary changes, or supplements can finally take root and hold.

The final step then is integration by turning regulation and rebuilding into a daily rhythm. We learn to notice early signs of imbalance and respond before a full flare. We continue to keep the body open to healing over the long term.

Fighting for the Second Half of Healing

My friend and I are walking this together. She brings her deep research on gut health. I bring the trauma-awareness and regulation tools. Neither of us are medical professionals but we are learning how to hold the whole picture when the system won't.

It's a lot of work and it's frustrating at times. It's also proof that even without official titles, people can reclaim their health by combining knowledge, intuition, and patience.

The Rooted Path doesn't replace medical care. It fills in what the system leaves out. It's not about rejecting doctors, but about recognizing that surviving the crisis is only half the job. True healing means tending the terrain afterward, so the body can stay well and resilient.

You cannot heal only the part of the body that hurts and expect lasting change. The whole system has to be considered. This includes the gut, hormones, immune function, nervous system, and the emotional terrain that holds it all.

The medical model will likely continue to focus on the crisis first. But we can choose to claim the second half of healing for ourselves, not as a replacement for medical care, but as its completion. I have included a Rooted Path Recovery Map in the resources section at the back of the book as a guide to help in your recovery.

Twenty Two

Everyday Stress & Anxiety

E veryday stress rarely arrives as a lightning bolt. More often, it seeps into your life in small, ordinary ways, the meeting that ran long, the sink full of dishes you swore you'd get to earlier, the traffic jam when you were already running late.

On their own, these moments don't seem like much. You sigh, you move on. But stacked together without release, they build into an invisible weight you carry through the day. You may not notice it until you find yourself snapping at someone you love, lying awake replaying conversations, or sinking into exhaustion that no amount of rest seems to touch.

The body is not designed to carry these small stresses endlessly. Each one triggers a miniature stress response: your adrenal glands release a quick burst of hormones, your heart rate ticks up, muscles brace. If another stressor arrives before the first has cleared, the nervous system never fully resets. It stays in a low-grade state of "almost alert," as if an app is running in the background, quietly draining your battery.

This is why "little things" matter. Your body does not measure stress by the size of the event but by frequency and recovery. A dozen minor activations without release can be just as taxing as one major event. Over time, the accumulation narrows your attention, heightens your reactivity, and leaves you living with a constant hum of tension.

That same hum is what fuels anxiety and overthinking. Stress that never completes its cycle can intensify into a restless current that floods the body. Anxiety raises the volume, every thought echoing louder, every possibility rushing forward.

Overthinking spins that current into endless loops: replaying conversations, anticipating worst-case scenarios, rehearsing what you'll say or do if the imagined thing ever comes true. These states are not character flaws. They are survival strategies the nervous system has practiced for so long that they've become traps, constant vigilance that never finds resolution.

The Rooted Path offers a way to break this loop, not by forcing the mind to be quiet, but by meeting the body where the charge lives. The first step is to catch the current early. Stress and anxiety are easiest to shift at the very beginning, before they have built momentum.

Notice the first signs: your shoulders creeping toward your ears, your jaw tightening, your breath caught high in your chest. Sometimes anxiety feels more like a flutter in the belly or a buzzing in the temples. Instead of following the thought, name the sensation. "My breath feels shallow." "There's a hum in my ribs." "My shoulders feel tight." This simple acknowledgment stops the snowball and brings you back into the body.

The second step is to allow that energy to transmute, to give it a different shape. Because stress often happens in the middle of busy days, this doesn't require a full ritual. Even a minute is enough. Use the elements as anchors: when you feel restless, imagine the heat of fire softening from a flickering flame into a steady ember.

When the day feels sticky or heavy, let water help you reset, sip slowly from a glass, run your hands under cool water, picture the weight washing through and away.

When anxiety leaves you ungrounded, return to earth, place your feet flat and press them into the ground until you feel your body settle. And when thoughts are racing, invite air, take a long inhale and exhale with a sigh, letting space open in the mind. You don't need to overthink which element to choose. Trust your body's first impulse.

The third step is integration, because stress lingers when the body isn't told that it's over. After your reset, pause for one more breath and mark the moment: This is new.

Some people like to pair this with a gesture, shaking out the hands, rolling the shoulders, or placing a hand on the chest. With anxiety especially, it helps to stay with the calmer sensation for a minute or two, letting the body memorize it as a new baseline. These small acts tell the nervous system, we are safe now.

The final step is embodiment, which shifts the way you live. The goal is not to eliminate stress or anxiety completely, but to change your relationship with them. Recovery becomes faster.

Your body learns it does not have to stay braced. You begin to speak without snapping, to listen without rehearsing every possible reply, to rest without guilt. You move through tasks without the rush in your chest, and you start noticing the joys in between, sunlight on the wall, the taste of your coffee, the sound of someone's laugh. Stress still comes, but it does not stay. Anxiety may arise, but it no longer commands you.

– A Story from the Path –

One friend used to believe he "handled stress well" because he didn't yell or panic.

But every night he collapsed onto the couch tense and drained, scrolling his phone to numb out.

Only when he began practicing micro resets did he realize how many small activations he'd been ignoring.

His favorite became the earth mini: pressing his feet into the floor, imagining roots. "It's like I can feel my brain unclench," he told me. Slowly, the weighted vest he thought was normal began to lift.

– Another Story from the Path –

A woman had lived with anxiety so long she thought of it as her personality.

Her mind raced constantly, sleep came in fragments, and she dreaded empty time.

At first, she found the activation step nearly impossible, noticing sensation felt foreign compared to tracking thoughts. But she kept trying. Her simple practice was three deep breaths by an open window, picturing the air clearing her mind.

Over months, she felt the hum in her chest before the spiral began, and she could choose to reset. "It's not that I never get anxious," she said, "it's that I finally have a way back.

I don't feel trapped in my head anymore."

This is why the Rooted Path works for stress and anxiety alike. Stress accumulates in the body until it hums. Anxiety fuels itself on that hum until it spins into endless thought. By meeting the charge directly, activating awareness, transmuting the energy, integrating the shift, embodying the reset, the loop breaks. The result is not a life without stress or thought, but a life where neither has to trap you. You learn to move with them, let them pass, and return to a steady ground you can trust.

Twenty Three

Food, Health, and Cravings

Our relationship with food is never just about food. Every bite carries a story of comfort, celebration, stress relief, habit, or even survival.

For some, eating is a daily act of nourishment and pleasure. For others, it's a constant negotiation between hunger, health goals, emotions, and cravings that seem to have a will of their own.

The Rooted Path meets you here not as a diet, not as a rigid plan, but as a way of noticing and shaping the energy that surrounds eating. Because whether you're reaching for a snack at midnight, skipping meals without realizing it, or eating past fullness because you "don't want to waste food," there's always an energetic current underneath the action.

When you learn to meet that current with awareness instead of judgment or autopilot, you create space for a different choice.

Why Food and Energy Are So Closely Linked

On the physical level, food is energy, literally. Your body breaks it down into glucose, fatty acids, and amino acids, turning it into fuel for every movement, thought, and heartbeat. This is basic metabolism.

On the emotional and energetic levels, food also plays other roles. Food can be a comfort, a way to soothe activation or numb discomfort. It can be a form of connection, meals shared with others become emotional anchors. Food can feel like a reward, a "treat" after a hard day or a success. In some cases, it can be a form of avoidance, eating to distract from feelings you'd rather not meet.

In Ayurveda, food is one of the primary ways we shape prana, the life force. Different foods can increase heaviness (tamas), stimulate activity (rajas), or promote clarity and balance (sattva). In Traditional Chinese Medicine, food is understood as qi in tangible form, carrying the qualities of the seasons, elements, and the land where it grew. Your relationship with food is, in many ways, a relationship with life itself.

The Three Layers of Food-Related Activation

Before you change a single bite, it helps to notice which layer of activation you're actually working with.

Physical hunger, your body genuinely needs fuel. This is the growling stomach, lightheadedness, or energy dip that comes from a long stretch without eating.

Emotional hunger, you're seeking a shift in state (comfort, distraction, celebration) whether your body needs fuel or not.

Patterned habit, you eat because it's "time," because it's there, or because it's what you've always done in this situation. The Rooted Path works with all three layers, but the approach is different for each.

Step 1 – Activate: Catching the Craving Early

A craving often starts subtly. You glance toward the kitchen. You think about the leftover dessert. You open the fridge "just to see." Instead of going on autopilot, pause and notice. Where do I feel this in my body? (Jaw? Stomach? Chest?) Does it feel like urgency or like a steady need? What's happening around me or inside me right now?

If you're physically hungry, honoring that hunger is part of the Path, meeting your body's needs without guilt. If it's emotional or patterned, this is where the work begins.

Step 2 – Transmute: Separating the Energy from the Food

This is not about "fighting the craving." Fighting usually makes it stronger. Instead, you meet the craving as energy and give it another channel. If the craving feels:

Hot and urgent → *Fire:* Place your hands on your belly, breathe into the heat, and imagine it softening into a steady ember.

Heavy and lingering → *Water:* Sip warm tea slowly, imagining it washing through the craving, carrying it onward.

Big and overwhelming → *Earth:* Stand barefoot or press your feet firmly into the floor. Imagine the craving's energy sinking down into the ground to be held.

Mental and looping → *Air:* Take three slow breaths, exhaling fully each time, and imagine the craving floating upward into space.

By giving the energy somewhere to go, you're not denying yourself, you're transforming the charge so you can decide more clearly whether eating right now is truly what you want.

Step 3 – Integrate: Choose From the New State

After transmuting, check again. Is my body still asking for food? If yes, what would feel nourishing and satisfying right now? If not, what was I really seeking? Comfort? Break? Connection?

This is where you make the choice from steadiness rather than from the pull of activation. Sometimes you'll still choose to eat the cake, and you'll enjoy it more because you're present with it. Sometimes you'll realize you wanted a glass of water, a walk, or a moment of quiet instead.

Step 4 – Embody: Building a Steady Food Relationship

Over time, these micro-moments of presence shift the whole way you relate to eating. You stop swinging between over-control and over-indulgence. Food stops being the enemy, the crutch, or the battleground. It becomes food again, fuel, pleasure, and connection without the extra weight of unprocessed energy.

You might notice that the cravings still come, but they feel less urgent. You can pause mid-meal and decide whether to keep eating without guilt. Emotional eating becomes a conscious choice instead of an automatic one.

This isn't about perfection. It's about building a rooted rhythm with food that leaves you feeling nourished, body, mind, and energy.

– A Story from the Path –

A friend used to reach for chocolate every time she felt stressed. "I knew I wasn't hungry," she told me, "but it was the fastest way to take the edge off."

When she started using the Path, she noticed that her craving for chocolate always came with a tight chest and restless hands, a fire energy. So she began putting her hands on her belly, breathing into the heat, and imagining it softening before deciding whether to eat.

Within weeks, she realized half the time she didn't actually want the chocolate. She wanted to move, stretch, or call a friend. And when she did eat it, she enjoyed it instead of inhaling it.

"It's like I got my choice back," she said. "Chocolate isn't in charge anymore."

When Health Goals Enter the Picture

If you're working toward a health change, healing your gut, balancing hormones, lowering inflammation, the Path becomes even more valuable. Dietary shifts often bring up resistance, grief, or rebellion, especially if certain foods carry emotional meaning.

Instead of trying to "willpower" through, you can meet the emotion underneath the craving. Transmute the energy first. Make the choice from your grounded state, honoring both your body's needs and your emotional truth.

This doesn't guarantee you'll follow your plan perfectly but it does mean you'll be making conscious choices instead of swinging between compliance and backlash.

Why This Matters Beyond the Plate

Food is one of the most direct, tangible ways we interact with energy every day. When you can meet cravings and eating patterns with presence, you're practicing the same skills you use for stress, relationships, and creative work.

You're learning to notice activation early, separate the charge from the action, and make choices from steadiness instead of urgency. That practice doesn't just change your meals, it changes your life.

Twenty Four

Rooted Relationships

Relationships are one of the most powerful mirrors we will ever face. They hold our deepest desires, our oldest wounds, our fiercest activations, and our most tender joys. Whether in the pull of attraction, the intimacy of romance, the daily challenges of parenting, or the quiet resonance of friendship and community, relationships continually invite us into deeper honesty with ourselves.

The Rooted Path does not remove these challenges. It doesn't promise ease, perfect harmony, or endless patience. What it does offer is a way to remain steady within them. A way to meet the surges of energy that relationships bring without losing yourself, betraying your values, or abandoning your ground.

Attraction as Life Force

Attraction is one of the most charged currents we experience. It can light the body with spark and possibility, but it can also disorient or overwhelm when it arrives at the "wrong" time or toward someone outside the boundaries of your commitments. In nervous system terms, attraction is full-spectrum activation. Heart rate shifts, breath quickens, neurochemicals surge, and your subtle field may expand toward the other person.

Attraction is not inherently a problem. It is a form of life force moving in response to resonance. On the Rooted Path, the first step is to name it without shame. This is attraction. I feel it here. From there, you can shape the energy rather than being ruled by it. Fire may steady heat into clarity, air may disperse restless fantasy, water may soften longing into compassion, and earth may ground desire into rootedness.

Transmutation here does not mean extinguishing attraction. It means guiding it into alignment with your values. Sometimes that looks like letting it inspire creativity or vitality in other areas of life. Sometimes it means pausing long enough to ask: does moving toward this person honor what matters most to me? Attraction, met with integrity, becomes a teacher rather than a trap.

Romance as a Mirror

Romantic love is often where our edges show most clearly. The early spark softens defenses and draws us into openness, but as the chemistry evens out, our old patterns resurface. A partner's silence might echo an old abandonment. Their tone might mirror a parent's sharpness.

Suddenly the charge in your body is not only about this moment but about every moment that felt like it before.

The next time you feel heat rising in your chest mid-conversation, pause for one slow inhale before you respond. Even that breath can open the door to a different choice.

The Rooted Path slows this chain reaction. In conflict, you pause to notice: My chest is hot. My shoulders are tight. My breath is shallow. Instead of speaking from the wound, you steady yourself with an elemental reset. Fire cools to embers. Water flows heaviness through. Earth roots your stance. Air clears the spiral. Only then do you return to speak, not silenced, but grounded enough that your words come from the present, not the past.

Relationships are not measured by the absence of conflict but by the presence of repair. On the Path, repair looks like owning your part without collapsing into shame, naming your process, and reaffirming your intention. Love here becomes a practice, not of avoiding the flood but of learning to navigate it together.

Parenting as Daily Practice

Parenting may be the most activating relationship of all. It stirs primal instincts, awakens inherited patterns, and demands constant adaptation. A child's meltdown in the grocery store or slammed bedroom door can pull you instantly into fight, flight, freeze, or fawn.

The Rooted Path gives you a way to pause before reacting. Notice the signal in your body: My throat is hot. My hands want to clench. Breathe into your feet, imagine roots, let the edge soften before responding. This isn't about never losing your cool, it's about showing your child how to return after rupture.

Children don't just listen to what you say; they feel your state. Your steadiness helps regulate theirs. Your dysregulation amplifies theirs. Co-regulation is not about controlling your child but offering them an anchor. By tending your own roots, you model regulation as a living language. When you falter, and you will, repair teaches them that relationships can hold imperfection and still thrive.

Resonance, Co-Regulation, and Holding Space

Relationships extend beyond romance and parenting. Every interaction, with friends, coworkers, clients, or strangers, is an exchange of state. Breath, posture, tone, and subtle energy are all signals our nervous systems read unconsciously. This is co-regulation: the way two systems tune to one another, for steadiness or for storm.

Resonance is what happens when we "tune" together, laughter spreading, grief shared, silence deepening in safety. It can heal, but it can also harm when trauma resonates unchecked. Awareness lets you choose: will I mirror this state, or will I hold a different one steady?

Holding space in this context means creating a field where another can meet themselves honestly without you collapsing into their storm. It is not absorbing their pain, nor rescuing them. It is standing rooted, like a lighthouse: open, present, but not swept away.

Energetic presence requires boundaries. Anchor your field with grounding and breath. Imagine your edges intact, light yet whole. When you feel another's energy press against yours, silently name it: This is theirs, not mine. Let it pass through the space you hold without taking it into your body.

When residue lingers, shake it off, wash your hands, step into sunlight, or breathe fresh air. These rituals signal to your system that the interaction is complete. You are clear again.

The Rooted Path in Relationships

Across attraction, romance, parenting, friendship, and community, the principles remain the same. Notice the charge. Shape it gently. Anchor the shift. Live from the steadier state.

Relationships will always stir currents. Desire, conflict, fear, joy, grief, these are the waves of human connection. The Rooted Path doesn't ask you to mute them. It invites you to meet them fully without being swept away.

When you do, attraction becomes creativity, conflict becomes growth, parenting becomes modeling, and co-regulation becomes healing. You stop abandoning yourself in connection, and instead discover that the deepest integrity is not in holding perfectly still, but in bending with the currents while remaining rooted.

Twenty Five

Rooted Work & Creativity

Work and creativity are two of the places where activation shows itself most vividly — and where we're often least equipped to meet it. In professional life, we face deadlines, difficult personalities, and constant communication under the pressure of "staying professional." In creative life, we face blocks, perfectionism, exhaustion, and the tender risk of bringing something unseen into the world.

In both, the Rooted Path offers a way to stay steady without suppressing yourself, to keep your energy flowing without letting it flood or collapse.

Work as a Field of Activation

Most workplaces operate under an unspoken contract: keep your emotions in check. Which often means: keep them hidden. But hidden charges don't vanish. They stack, the sharp email, the interrupted meeting, the tense exchange with your supervisor.

The mask you wear to stay "professional" may protect your reputation, but it doesn't protect your body. Stored charge shows up as headaches, tight muscles, restless sleep, or a slow erosion of motivation.

The Rooted Path doesn't ask you to throw the mask away. It gives you a way to tend to what's underneath, so the mask doesn't become your whole face.

Practice in Work Settings: The next time a small stressor arises, a snappy message, a meeting that drags on, a sudden deadline, pause just long enough to notice your body. Two deep breaths before you reply. A conscious unclenching of your jaw when someone else is speaking. Press your feet into the ground beneath the table and feel the weight of your body supported.

These are invisible gestures to everyone else, but to your nervous system they are signals: this charge is seen, and it doesn't need to stay lodged here. Over time, these micro-resets prevent the steady accumulation that turns small stress into chronic burnout.

Creativity and the Nature of Blocks

Creative work holds its own challenges. To create is to risk, to pull something from the unseen into the seen. Which means that when activation rises, the channel clogs. We call it a "block," but really it's a knot of energy.

Some knots are hot with urgency and perfectionism. Others are heavy with grief or fatigue. Some are scattered with distraction. Others hide in the fog, where you can't even feel desire to create. The Rooted Path reframes blocks not as failure, but as signals. A block is energy asking to move.

Practice in Creative Work: When you sit down to make something and feel the old familiar stall, resist the urge to label it "block" and force yourself through. Instead, name what's actually happening in sensation language: heat in my chest, heaviness in my shoulders, thoughts racing.

Then, choose an elemental gesture to shift it. Write your fear on paper and burn it (fire). Place your hands in cool water to let the weight disperse (water). Step outside barefoot or hold a grounding object (earth). Breathe three long exhales as though clearing clouds (air). Afterward, pause to notice how your body feels different, perhaps a little more open and a little less urgent. This pause is not wasted time. It is the moment the knot begins to loosen.

Professionals and the Weight of Others

For those in helping or high-contact roles, therapists, teachers, coaches, leaders, first responders, activation is multiplied. You don't just carry your own charges, you sit in the presence of others' every day. Clients, students, and colleagues feel not just your words, but your state.

Burnout here often isn't caused by what you do, but by what you hold without releasing. Compassion fatigue, cynicism, numbing, headaches, or the quiet dread of the work you once loved, these are all signs of charge carried too long.

Practice for Professionals: Between interactions, give yourself a 60-second ritual. Step into the hallway or pause before your next call. Close your eyes. Choose one element to work with.

Imagine the tension in your chest cooling into a steady ember (fire). Place your palms on the desk and feel the weight drain into the surface (earth). Wash your hands slowly, as though rinsing away what isn't yours (water). Open a window and take three full exhales, letting the stale air carry the charge away (air). Anchor the shift with one small gesture, a hand to your chest, a whispered vow, this moment is new.

In time, these rituals become part of your professional hygiene, clearing the residue before it stacks into depletion.

The Shared Thread

Work, creativity, and professional service all ask the same thing: that you bring your energy forward in visible, often vulnerable ways. And all three are easily hijacked when charge builds unchecked.

The Rooted Path doesn't promise ease in these spaces. But it does give you a map. To catch the activation. To transmute it quietly, even invisibly. To integrate and reset before it stacks. To embody a steadiness that others can feel.

When you do, work doesn't drain you as deeply. Creativity doesn't abandon you as easily. Professional life doesn't erode you as quickly. Instead, each becomes a place where you can show up fully human, rooted, steady, and still able to create, serve, and lead with integrity.

There will be times when you still put on the mask. At work. In front of family. In moments where it feels safer to hide your trembling or your rage. That's not failure. That's survival.

What matters is that you know it's a mask. That you remember what lives beneath it, and you tend to that life quietly, even if no one else sees. A mask that forgets itself becomes a cage. A mask that remembers itself can be set down. Masks are temporary. You are not.

Twenty Six

Building Your Personal Toolkit

A t a certain point in every person's Rooted Path journey, they realize they cannot rely on sheer willpower alone. Awareness and intention are essential, but in the middle of a storm, when the charge is high, the nervous system is on alert, and old patterns are calling, it helps to have something you can reach for.

This is where your toolkit comes in. A personal toolkit is not just a box of "calm down" tricks. It is a living collection of practices, objects, and rituals that meet you exactly where you are and help you step into the Rooted Path in real time. It is both practical and sacred. Something you can touch, hear, smell, see, and feel that reminds you of the path you've chosen, even when you're standing in the doorway of old habits.

My First Toolkit Moment

When I first began walking this path, fear was my constant companion. It wasn't the kind of fear you could name in one sentence. It was layered, a deep, almost cellular fear born of past trauma, the kind that lived in my body even when my mind thought I was "over it."

One of the first things I did was cleanse my entire home. I moved slowly from room to room with intention, clearing out stagnant energy and opening the space for something new. This wasn't just "decluttering," it was a physical and energetic reset.

When that was complete, I performed a fire release ritual. I wrote down the things I was ready to let go of, fears, patterns, and echoes of the past that no longer belonged in my present. I read them out loud, not as an act of rage, but as a vow to release. Then I burned them, watching the flames consume the paper and feeling something in me shift.

That ritual became my first anchor. Every time fear surged in those early months, I could close my eyes and remember the smell of smoke, the sound of paper curling in the fire, the way the air felt afterward was lighter, clearer, more open. It gave my nervous system a memory of release to lean on.

The Bridge Between Then and Now

Over time, fear still visited but I had a bridge now. When it came, I reached for stones, especially black tourmaline for grounding and amethyst for calm. I paired them with a mantra I'd chosen. Just some simple words that reminded my body of safety and my mind of clarity. I would hold the stone, repeat the mantra, and breathe until the charge began to soften.

These tools didn't erase the fear instantly, but they gave me a way through it. Each time I used them, I noticed something important, the fear didn't stay as long. It didn't grip as hard. And slowly, the visits became fewer and farther between.

Today, I rarely feel that fear at all. When it does come, it is minimal. A whisper instead of a roar, and I feel stronger, more confident, more rooted than I ever did in those early days. That's the deeper purpose of a toolkit: not just to help you survive the moment, but to change your baseline so you need it less and less.

What a Toolkit Really Is

A toolkit is not a sign you are weak. It's proof that you are willing to meet yourself where you are. Think of it as the bridge between knowing the Rooted Path and living it. In the beginning, you might need to reach for your tools often. Every time a charge rises, every time your system begins to spiral. Over time, the use becomes more intuitive. Some tools will fall away because you no longer need them and others will become so ingrained you don't even think of them as "tools" anymore, they're just part of who you are.

Before we talk about specific tools, it's important to understand the principles that make them effective.

Core Principles for Building Your Toolkit

They should be personal. If you don't resonate with crystals, you won't use them. If music shifts your mood faster than anything else, make it part of your core set. Choose what feels alive and real to you.

They should engage the senses. Your nervous system responds to sensory input, touch, sound, scent, sight, movement. The more senses a tool engages, the more powerfully it can help shift your state.

They should be easy to access. If a tool is buried in the back of a closet or takes 20 minutes to set up, you won't use it when you need it most.

They should be adaptable. Life doesn't always give you quiet space and privacy. Some tools need to work in public, in conversation, in the car. Build options for different environments.

They should remind you of who you are. Every tool should be a thread back to your center, not a distraction from what you feel.

The Toolkit Resources

On my own journey and through the resources I share on my website, I've found certain categories of tools to be especially powerful. These are not just methods I've studied, they're living practices I've used and seen work for others. You can explore them as-is or adapt them into your own language and rhythm.

Ayurveda — Ayurveda offers grounding rituals tailored to your constitution and current state. Whether it's sipping warm spiced tea for comfort, doing self-massage with warm oil, or adjusting your daily rhythm to match the sun, these practices help your body feel safe enough to shift energy.

Herbalism — Plants carry their own energy and medicine. Chamomile to soften tension, tulsi for uplifting, lemon balm for soothing the heart, these are not just physical remedies, but allies for your emotional state. Herbal teas, tinctures, and even the act of brewing can become part of your ritual.

Crystals — Stones act as physical anchors. Black tourmaline for protection, rose quartz for self-compassion, clear quartz for clarity, each can serve as a touchstone in moments of activation. Holding them in your hand gives your body something to focus on as you work with the charge.

Sound — Sound moves energy. It can be as simple as humming, playing a singing bowl, or listening to a song that shifts your state. The vibration bypasses the thinking mind and works directly with the body's rhythm.

Mantra — A few words, spoken with intention, can be a lifeline. "I am safe." "I return to center." "I choose peace." Choose phrases that feel true in your bones, not just your mind.

Meditation — Meditation doesn't have to mean sitting still for hours. Even two minutes of mindful breathing, or placing awareness on a single sensation, can be enough to keep you on the path when a charge rises.

Breath — Your breath is always with you and it is one of the fastest ways to influence your nervous system. Slow exhales, box breathing, or simply pausing to notice the breath can create the space you need to respond instead of react.

Energy — the undercurrent of every experience. It moves beneath emotion, sensation, and thought. Learning to notice it is like learning a second language your body has always spoken.

Ritual — presence made visible. It is how we mark a moment as sacred, not because of what it looks like, but because of the intention within it. Lighting a candle, placing your hand on your heart, whispering a name, stirring herbs into water. These are not just actions, they are invitations. Ritual gives your nervous system something to trust, a rhythm to return to.

Creativity — Drawing, painting, writing, singing, creative acts give energy a place to go. They don't have to be "good" to be effective. They just have to be honest.

Movement — Walking, stretching, yoga, dancing, shaking, movement helps energy complete its cycle. Even subtle shifts, like rolling your shoulders or swaying in your seat, can release tension.

Writing — Journaling can help you name the charge without drowning in it. Sometimes the act of putting words on paper is enough to loosen energy's grip.

Nature — The natural world is a master of regulation. Standing barefoot on the earth, listening to water, watching clouds move, nature invites your body back into its own rhythm.

Connection — We are wired for resonance. Talking to someone who can hold space without judgment, sitting in the presence of a calm friend, or even placing a hand on your own heart with compassion, these are all forms of connection that bring us back to center.

How to Build Yours

Start with what works now. Make a list of things that already help you feel more steady, even in small ways.

Choose one tool from each sense. Something to touch, something to hear, something to smell, something to see, something to move with.

Create a portable version. A small bag or pouch with a stone, a tiny vial of essential oil, a folded piece of paper with your mantra, and earbuds for music.

Practice before you need it. Don't wait for a crisis to try your tools. Use them when you're calm so your body associates them with safety. Evolve as you grow. Some tools will fade. Others will deepen. Your toolkit should change as you do.

Twenty Seven

A Closing Whisper

There is not a single moment when the Rooted Path declares, you've arrived. No gates swing open. No trumpets sound. No certificate appears in your hands. Instead, there is the quiet knowing that you are not where you began.

You breathe, and the breath carries more space than it used to. You feel a charge rise in your body, and instead of bracing against it, you turn toward it. Not perfectly, not every time, but often enough that it matters.

You've grown roots here, even if you didn't notice them growing. This is the truth no one tells you at the beginning: the Path is not a straight road with a final destination. It's a spiral you will walk again and again, meeting the same places from different angles, each time with a little more light in your hands.

The Return

If you've walked with me through these pages, you've learned the steps.

Activate — to notice when the current rises, to name the shift without judgment.

Transmute — to meet the energy where it is and guide it into a new shape, using your intention, your senses, your tools, your breath.

Integrate — to let the new state land in your body, sealing it so it becomes part of who you are.

Embody — to live the Path without needing the map in your hands, carrying it in your bones instead.

You've learned the language of energy within you, around you, and between us. You've walked with the elements. You've held your own fear and found that it didn't break you. You've begun to see that even the heaviest currents can be shifted, not by force, but by presence.

Now comes the part that belongs only to you, the return. The daily practice of choosing again. The quiet agreement to keep walking, even when the fog rolls in, even when the hum feels far away.

What You Carry Now

By now, you have more than information. You carry memories in your body of moments when you stayed one breath longer instead of reacting, when you held the heat until it softened, when you let yourself weep and found that the weeping itself was medicine.

You carry a toolkit, whether it sits in a pouch by your bed or lives entirely in your mind, stones, mantras, herbs, sounds, breaths, movements that meet you in the moment.

You carry the elemental compass, a way of feeling your way back to center without needing to think about it. And perhaps most important, you carry the truth that your energy is not your enemy. It is part of you, part of life. It is a current you can learn to ride.

You Will Forget, And That's Okay

There will be days you lose the Path. You'll react before you remember to pause. You'll shut down when you mean to stay open. You'll go hours or days before you realize you've been living in fog.

This is not failure, this is being human. The Path does not punish you for forgetting, it waits. The moment you remember... in the middle of washing dishes, in the car, in the quiet before sleep, you can return. You do not have to start over. You are always starting from where you are, and that is enough.

The Ripples

Never underestimate what your practice does for others. When you hold your center in a hard conversation, you are offering an unspoken invitation for others to do the same. When you let your grief soften into compassion, you become a place where others can rest. When you shift your own energy, you shift the field you share with everyone around you.

These ripples are not always visible. You may never know the full reach of your presence. But someone will breathe easier because you stood rooted when it would have been easier to collapse. Someone will feel safer in your presence because you met your own charge with care. Someone will learn, without words, that it's possible to live another way.

When the Path Feels Distant

There will be seasons when your practice feels effortless, when the steps come easily, and you can feel the hum of connection without reaching for it. There will also be seasons when the Path feels far away, when nothing seems to work, and every tool feels dull in your hands.

In those times, return to the smallest thing. One breath. One stone in your palm. One step outside to feel the wind on your face. Do not demand a full return in one day.

Let yourself be met where you are. The Path is not about perfection. It's about returning, again and again, until returning is your nature.

If you remember nothing else from this book, remember this, you are not at the mercy of what rises in you. You have the capacity to meet it, to hold it, to shape it. Your energy is not a threat to be erased, it is a living current you can guide. Every time you do, you are not just changing yourself, you are shaping the field we all share.

You are not alone in this. There are others walking their own Rooted Path, weaving their own roots, tending their own fields. You may never meet them, but you will feel them in the ease that enters a room, in the quiet that settles in your chest, in the unspoken knowing that someone else is holding the light with you.

Walking Further Together

You've now walked through the roots, branches, and seasons of this path. You may be feeling more steady, more connected or you may simply know, in your bones, that there is more to explore.

This work doesn't have to be walked alone. Sometimes we need a guide to help us see what we can't yet see, to hold space while we step into the parts of ourselves we've been avoiding, or to remind us we are safe enough to keep going. If you're ready for more, there are two ways we can keep walking together.

One-on-One Sessions — I offer personalized sessions for those who want to work directly with the Tree of Becoming method. These sessions are tailored to your pace, your history, and your goals. Whether you're navigating daily stress, working through long-held patterns, or exploring your awakening journey.

Practitioner Certification — If you feel called to guide others, you can train to become a certified Tree of Becoming: Rooted Path

Practitioner. This program will teach you the full framework, give you the tools to hold safe, effective space for others, and connect you with a community of practitioners walking this same path.

Whether you continue on your own, with me, or with another guide, remember, you are already on the path. The roots are already growing and you have everything you need to keep becoming.

So here is my closing whisper for you, as you step from these pages back into the world... May your roots grow deep enough to hold you in any storm. May your breath be the bridge between fear and peace. May you meet your own currents with the same care you would offer a child. May you remember that you are part of a larger hum, a field that carries us all. And may you walk this Path not as a task to be completed, but as a way of being. A quiet, steady return to yourself, over and over again. The Rooted Path is not hidden anymore. It is here. It is yours... It is you.

Resources

The Rooted Path grew from my lived experience, but I also drew inspiration from wisdom traditions and modern research that helped me put language to what I was discovering. If you'd like to go deeper, these are some beautiful places to begin.

Ayurveda – *Ayurveda: The Science of Self-Healing by Dr. Vasant Lad*

Polyvagal Theory – *Anchored: How to Befriend Your Nervous System Using Polyvagal Theory by Deb Dana*

Somatic Healing – *Waking the Tiger: Healing Trauma by Peter Levine*

Trauma & the Body – *The Body Keeps the Score by Bessel van der Kolk*

Energy & Mind-Body Practices – *The Untethered Soul by Michael A. Singer*

Research on Coherence – HeartMath Institute: Consciousness, Human Heart, and Global Energetic Field Environment *https://www.heartmath.org/research/research-library/coherence/consciousness-human-heart-and-global-energetic-field-environment/*

About the Author

Brittanie McQueen is an artist, healer, and writer whose work lives at the intersection of soul, body, and Earth. Through her practice, EcoBound Holistics, and the living frameworks she has created, she guides others through sacred thresholds of remembrance, healing, and becoming.

A lifelong artist and printmaker, Brittanie believes that creativity is not a luxury but a way back to the self, a bridge between the visible and unseen. Her own path of trauma recovery, spiritual awakening, and embodied re-rooting revealed a quiet truth: within each surge of emotion lies not only pain, but a pulse of possibility. The body remembers. Healing is already seeded within.

Her purpose is to help others in transition — those awakening, unraveling, becoming. She holds space for those navigating thresholds, the in-between, the not-yet, the remembering.

She supports others in reconnecting to their creative nature, intuitive guidance, and the sacred wisdom of their bodies. Through writing, breath, energy, ritual, and tools made by hand, her work is an invitation to come home to the self and to the Earth.

Her offerings are woven with reverence for the natural world, the wisdom of the body, and the power of presence. Through words, sacred tools, rituals, and energy work, she calls others home to themselves and to the living Earth.

When not writing, painting, or tending to her work, she can be found walking barefoot under trees, gathering stones, or sharing quiet moments with those she loves. She believes healing is not a solitary act, but a rippling return to wholeness that touches families, communities, and the wider web of life.

The Rooted Path is more than a book. It is her offering, her remembrance, her invitation to walk the spiral home, to carry the ripple outward, to become whole in mind, body, and soul.

www.ingramcontent.com/pod-product-compliance
Lightning Source LLC
Chambersburg PA
CBHW021157130626
46554CB00005B/1865